ANTONIO GRAMSCI

ANTONIO GRAMSCI
by Antonio A. Santucci

Translated by Graziella Di Mauro
with Salvatore Engel-Di Mauro

Preface by Eric J. Hobsbawm
Foreword by Joseph A. Buttigieg
Editor's note by Lelio La Porta

MONTHLY REVIEW PRESS
New York

Orignally published as *Antonio Gramsci, 1897–1937*

by Sellerio editore, Palermo, Italy, © 2005 by Sellerio editore

English translation published by Monthly Review Press

Santucci, Antonio A.

 [Antonio Gramsci, 1891-1937. English]

 Antonio Gramsci / by Antonio A. Santucci; translated by Graziella Di Mauro, with Salvatore Engel-Di Mauro; preface by Eric J. Hobsbawm ; foreword by Joseph A. Buttigieg ; editor's note by Lelio La Porta.

  p. cm.

 Includes bibliographical references and index.

 ISBN 978-1-58367-210-5 (pbk.) – ISBN 978-1-58367-211-2 (cloth)

 1. Gramsci, Antonio, 1891–1937. 2. Communism–Italy. I. Di Mauro, Graziella. II. Engel-Di Mauro, Salvatore. III. Title.

 HX289.7.G73S2413 2010

 320.53'2092–dc22

 [B]

                                    2010010488

Monthly Review Press

146 West 29th Street, Suite 6W

New York, New York 10001

www.monthlyreview.org

www.MRzine.org

5 4 3 2 1

Contents

Preface

by Eric J. Hobsbawm

Among the most distinguished intellectuals of the twentieth century, perhaps no other left his own body of work upon his death in a less accessible form than Antonio Gramsci. And yet, this has not hindered him from becoming perhaps the most well-known and influential Italian thinker of the century. This is due primarily to the two scholars who dedicated a large portion of their lives to methodically organizing and analyzing his works: Valentino Gerratana and Antonio A. Santucci. Both of them are no longer with us; Gerratana's passing was followed by the unexpected loss of Santucci, his collaborator and—in reality—his successor as the foremost expert in Gramscian studies. Santucci was only fifty-four, and his loss was both tragic and the cause of much regret. How much might we yet have expected from this man of remarkable ability, who combined solid scholarship in numerous fields in the history of political theory with an ironic and uncompromising intelligence and a witty temperament tinged just slightly with a pinch of melancholy! Beyond being the predominant philological scholar of Gramscian texts, Santucci was renowned for his critical analysis of Gramsci and, through the lens of Gramsci's

Prison Notebooks, of the historical period in which he participated. Santucci, therefore, should be remembered both for his philological scholarship and his own personal work represented by various essays, and especially for his thoughts on the continued importance of Gramsci in a world "Without Communism."[1]

Antonio Santucci and Antonio Gramsci: An Open Dialogue

by Joseph A. Buttigieg

Antonio Santucci's massive contribution to the study and dissemination of Gramsci's work and thought took so many forms that it cannot be succinctly characterized, much less adequately described, in a few pages. The most tangible and readily accessible aspect of Santucci's Gramscian activities is, of course, the large body of publications he produced; his name appears in over 250 items listed in the enormous *Bibliografia gramsciana* that John Cammett compiled over the years. By itself, a bibliographical list provides only the faint contours of the author's labors: it tells us when, where, and by whom his books and articles were published. From these sparse data one can also glean some other interesting information: Santucci's writings were unusually diverse in nature, he wrote for many different types of readers, and he was sought out by the editors of books and periodicals in many foreign countries, including Spain, France, Austria, Hungary, Finland, Brazil, Chile and Japan. What the bibliography does not—indeed, cannot—provide is a qualitative assessment of Santucci's works. Only those who proceed from the bibliography to the shelves of the library to retrieve and read the texts themselves can appreciate his philological, hermeneutical, and critical skills; the rigor and depth of the research he conducted into every aspect of Gramsci's life and work; and the remarkable stylistic versatility that enabled him to pitch every single thing he wrote to the readers he was addressing.

The bibliography of Santucci's publications, furthermore, tells us nothing about the impact he had (and will continue to have) on the work of countless other individuals. Nor does it record the names of the many scholars and students he helped and advised both formally and informally over the course of two decades. The same is true of the conferences he organized, the seminars and symposia at which he talked, and the publications of works by other scholars that he enabled—most notably, Eugenio Garin's *Con Gramsci* (1997); there is no instrument with which to weigh the importance and significance of their effects on the various currents of Gramscian scholarship both in Italy and abroad. Santucci's influence has not always left visible traces; yet, it runs silently through much that has been written on Gramsci since the late 1980s, when he started to emerge as one of the most reliable and knowledgeable experts on the great Sardinian's life and work.

Through his philologically scrupulous editions of *L'Ordine Nuovo* [The New Order] (with Valentino Gerratana), *Letters: 1908-1926*, and *Letters from Prison*, Santucci provided scholars and students reliable access to some of Gramsci's most important writings—these are definitive texts and will remain so for the foreseeable future. His other, more popular, editions of Gramsci's writings have been of equal and perhaps even greater importance to the dissemination of Gramsci's thought on a broader cultural terrain. The paperback edition of the *Letters from Prison* (published as a supplement of *l'Unità*, January 24, 1988), the small selection of journalistic writings, *Piove, governo ladro!* [It's rain-ing, damned government!] (1996), and *Le opere. La prima antologia di tutti gli scritti* [Writings: First selection from the complete works] (1997), to mention just three examples, intro-duced Gramsci's writings and made them accessible to a huge spectrum of readers and to students for whom they would have otherwise remained "classics" entombed in libraries among the many rows of heavy, intimidating tomes accumulating dust.

This is not to say that Santucci did not consider Gramsci a "classic." In fact, Santucci's first book on Gramsci opens pre-cisely with a discussion of his status as a classic; but he is con-cerned lest Gramsci might suffer the same fate as many other clas-sics that are universally revered, frequently cited, but rarely read, except out of a sense of scholastic or cultural obligation. That is why Santucci repeatedly and consistently attempted to bring his readers into direct contact with Gramsci's texts; he did this not only with his editions, but also in his books and essays of inter-pretation and analysis. Underlying them all is the conviction that the dialogue with Gramsci can be kept alive through his texts. For Santucci, then, Gramsci is simultaneously a classic and currently relevant. What distinguishes Gramsci from certain other classics, in other words, is that his writings invite the reader, even today, to become involved in an active—one could even say participatory—encounter with ideas and lines of thinking which, in the case of the *Prison Notebooks*, remain always in a fluid process of elabora-tion, reformulation, revision, amplification, etc. This is quite dif-ferent from readings of classic texts carried out from a detached and fundamentally disinterested vantage point—readings that are conditioned sometimes by the closed, perfected form of the clas-sic text itself and, at other times, by the Olympian stance adopted by the critic or scholar.

In his notes on literary criticism Gramsci draws a sharp con-trast between Francesco De Sanctis's militant criticism animated by the "impassioned fervor of a committed person who has firm moral and political convictions" and Benedetto Croce's posture (which was really a calculated pose) of "superior serenity" and an "indulgence full of bonhomie." He leaves no doubt as to his preference: "the type of literary criticism suitable to historical materialism is offered by De Sanctis, not by Croce" (Q, 23, §3). These observations are indicative of how Gramsci approached not only literary masterpieces (such as Manzoni's *The Betrothed*) but also certain classic texts of philosophy and political theory. One need only look at the very large block of notes on Machiavelli to see how deeply Gramsci involves himself in the interpretation of the Florentine's works; how his reading, while always attentive to the historical specificity of the original texts, leads him to an illuminating examination of the relations of power in the modern epoch (which, in turn, enables him to further develop and deepen his concept of hegemony), and to a series of reflections on the requirements of a political strategy adequate to his own times. Gramsci's reading of Machiavelli's *Prince* is an exemplary hermeneutical operation that cautiously avoids instrumentalizing the text even while "translating" it into a modern idiom. In his treatment of the *Prince*, Gramsci shows how a text can be simultaneously classic and relevant to the present time.

It would be futile, however, to search Gramsci's text for a ready-made formula of interpretation that would make every classic relevant to one's own historical conjuncture. Indeed, such a way of reading is sometimes neither possible nor desirable. This does not mean that a classic should be consigned to oblivion (as some militant cultural theorists have argued) simply because it embodies and expresses a *weltanschauung* that is incommensurable with the present reader's conception of the world. Rather, a classic that is not or cannot be made relevant to the present time could—indeed should—still be admired for its intrinsic qualities, even if only dispassionately. Gramsci makes some interesting remarks about this in his letter of 1 June 1931 to his wife Julia:

Who reads Dante with love? Doddering professors who make a religion of some poet or writer and perform strange philological rituals in his honor. I think that a modern and intelligent person ought to read the classics in general with a certain "detachment," that is, only for their aesthetic values, while "love" implies agreement with the ideological content of the poem; one loves one's "own" poet, one "admires" the artist "in general." Aesthetic admiration can be accompanied by a certain "civic" contempt, as in the case of Marx's attitude toward Goethe.

It is, of course, much easier to retain an attitude of detached admiration vis-à-vis a work of art than when dealing with a work of political philosophy. Thus, for example, a politically conservative American who "loves" Tocqueville would find it almost impossible to resist consigning Marx to eternal oblivion, even though *Das Kapital* is as much a classic as *Democracy in America*; and, needless to say, it is no accident that in the current conservative cultural-political atmosphere Tocqueville's best-known work is regarded as a paradigmatic example of a classic text that is unquestionably relevant to the present time. More often than not, though, the perception that Tocqueville's classic text has remained relevant stems from simplistic, ahistorical readings of *Democracy in America* that totally ignore the specific historical situation and political orientation of its author. This says nothing about the naïvety of treating the twenty-first century's only superpower as if its economic, social, and political structures are the same, in essence, as those observed by Tocqueville in the early 1830s. This manner of reading a classic uncritically from the perspective of the present has nothing in common with the procedures of interpretation and "translation" that characterize Gramsci's approach to Machiavelli. What it calls to mind, instead, are the crude efforts that have been made time and again to appropriate classic texts and instrumentalize them for crude and immediate political purposes. (Mussolini's edition of *Il Principe* is one of the most notorious examples of this phenomenon.)

Gramsci's work has not been exempted from instrumental (mis)interpretations and (mis)appropriations, despite the fact that the *Prison Notebooks* contain several explicit warnings against textual manipulation and hermeneutical dishonesty. In one very well known and frequently cited note, he wrote:

> "Importuning the texts." In other words, when out of zealous attachment to a thesis, one makes texts say more than they really do. This error of philological method occurs also outside of philology, in studies and analyses of all aspects of life. In terms of criminal law, it is analogous to selling goods at lesser weight and of different quality than had been agreed upon, but it is not considered a crime unless the will to deceive is glaringly obvious. But don't negligence and incompetence deserve to be sanctioned—if not a judicial sanction, at least an intellectual and moral sanction? (Q6, §198)

Gramsci's own philological rigor has not safeguarded his text from distortions by careless and incompetent readers. Some of the abuses of Gramsci's work can also be attributed to "the will to deceive." In many cases, unscrupulous and instrumental readings of Gramsci have made him appear relevant, particularly when he has been used to lend authority to or legitimize a specific political position or ideological tendency. From the other end of the spectrum, some prominent conservatives in the U.S. have been propagating the notion that "Gramscism" is very much alive today; in their eyes, Gramsci is the master theoretician and strategist of a resilient anti-capitalist, anti-democratic political current that has survived the communist debacle of 1989 and that, even now, represents an imminent threat to the political, social, and cultural *status quo*. In other words, Gramsci has often been made to look topical on false grounds and for the wrong reasons by putative admirers as well as by those who seek to demonize him.

For a while, it was possible to excuse certain misreadings and misappropriations of Gramsci on the grounds that the fragmentary and incomplete nature of his major text, the *Prison Notebooks*, coupled with the philologically problematic procedures employed by the editors of the thematically organized first edition, made multiple interpretations inevitable. The critical edition of 1975, meticulously edited by Valentino Gerratana, with its faithful transcription of the text as it appears in the manuscript, was expected to shed new light on Gramsci's massive opus, clarify at least some of its perceived ambiguities, reveal its internal structures or bring into relief the author's processes of composition, and thus make it possible to arrive at more reliable and stable interpretations of its contents. Some serious scholars have made excellent use of Gerratana's edition and arrived at a much better understanding of the trajectory of Gramsci's thought, a fuller comprehension of his concepts (including those about which so much had already been written, such as hegemony and civil society), and a realization that hitherto overlooked elements of the notebooks (such as the notes on the history of subaltern social groups and on Lorianism) provide valuable starting points for new research and theoretical elaboration. Unfortunately, however, these admirable developments in Gramscian philology have not displaced old, ingrained habits; all too often Gramsci's text continues to be treated as little more than a repository of phrases that are plucked out of their context to reinforce theses and lend authority to theories and critical practices that have little in common with, when they do not actually contradict, crucial aspects of his thought. The current fashionable discourse on global civil society is a case in point. Gramsci's assertion that "the search for the leitmotiv, the rhythm of the thought, is more important than single, isolated quotations" (Q4, §1) has failed to inhibit the practice of fishing in his text for single phrases or even paragraphs to embellish just about any kind of argument.

In reality, there is no legitimate excuse for the many self-serving and polemical uses to which Gramsci's writings have been subjected. Long before work on the complete critical edition of the *Prison Notebooks* had even begun, the most perspicacious readers of the thematic edition of the notebooks realized that their fragmentariness and incompletion could not be attributed solely to the atrocious conditions under which they were composed. They also realized that the fragmentariness and incompletion of Gramsci's text should not be used as a pretext to rearrange its various parts, fill its lacunae, and transform it into a systematic exposition of a fully worked-out theory. Eugenio Garin, for example, in a superb essay written as far back as 1958—"Gramsci e la cultura italiana," which is reprinted in *Letture di Gramsci* (1987) edited by Antonio Santucci—noted that the coherence of Gramsci's work is to be found in the recurrence of certain themes, issues, and preoccupations rather than in some underlying or overarching explanatory system. Among the passages he cites, two in particular stand out. One of them occurs in the course of Gramsci's critique of Bukharin's systematization of historical materialism: "There are those who believe that science must absolutely mean 'system,' and therefore they construct all kinds of systems that have only the mechanical outward appearance of a system" (Q7, §29). The other passage appears in a discussion of one of Croce's minor philosophical works: "Dissolution of the concept of a closed and fixed—and thus pedantic and abstruse—philosophical 'system'; affirmation that philosophy must resolve the problems that from time to time the historical process brings forth as it unfolds. Systematicity is to be sought in the internal consistency and productive sweep of each particular solution, not in some external architectural structure" (Q10, I, §4).

Always suspicious of grand explanatory schemes—and disdainful of those "who believe that they possess in a few brief and

stereotyped formulas the key to open all doors" (Q23, § 3)—
Gramsci repeatedly stressed the importance of paying attention
to phenomena in all their particularity and specificity. Pages and
pages of his notebooks are filled with notes on specific articles
from a wide range of journals, jottings on seemingly marginal
events, brief observations on some historical detail or another,
etc. Gramsci did not set out to explain historical reality armed
with some full-fledged concept, such as hegemony; rather, he
examined the minutiae of concrete social, economic, cultural and
political relations as they are lived by individuals in their specific
historical circumstances and, gradually, he acquired an increasingly complex understanding of how hegemony operates in many
diverse ways and under many aspects within the capillaries of
society. In the introduction to his edition of the *Letters from
Prison*, Santucci draws attention to Gramsci's impatience with
abstractions and generalizations by quoting from his letter of
November 19, 1928, to Julia:

> Books and magazines only offer general ideas, sketches (more or
> less successful) of general currents in the world's life, but they
> cannot give the immediate, direct, vivid impression of the lives of
> Peter, Paul, and John, of single, real individuals, and unless one
> understands them one cannot understand what is being univer-
> salized and generalized.

Gramsci's unwavering focus on the specific and the particular
and his constant yearning to be in close touch with the reality of
individual human existence are symptomatic of another distinctive aspect of his life and work: namely, the inseparability of his
theoretical work from his practical political activity. There has
always been a very strong tendency among readers of Gramsci to
regard the *Prison Notebooks* as a self-sufficient, isolated or
autonomous text. This is especially evident in the widespread
practice of separating the pre-prison writings from the *Notebooks*,

as if the two bodies of work belong to two separate phases of Gramsci's life. In more recent scholarly treatments of all of Gramsci's writings, their relation to his activities as a member (and subsequently as leader) of a political party receive scant attention. To be sure, Gramsci's arrest and imprisonment represent a real break or separation from his previous mode of existence. Yet, there are many important continuities between the political activist and the isolated prisoner that, if obscured or ignored, would seriously diminish the resonance of his work as well as his special significance as a historical figure. In his writings, Antonio Santucci insists repeatedly that the political activist and the intellectual are one and the same in Gramsci. Indeed, Santucci's Gramsci has many of the same characteristics that Gramsci attributed to Marx: "a nonsystematic thinker, with a personality in whom theoretical and practical activity are indissolubly intertwined, and with an intellect in continuous creation and perpetual movement" (Q4, §1).

It would seem that the most pronounced and distinctive characteristics of Gramsci's life and work—his adherence to a political movement that has all but disappeared, his preference for specificity and particularity over universal philosophy and totalizing theory, and the fragmentary, incomplete nature of what Togliatti aptly called his "literary legacy"—should consign him to the ash heap of history. Paradoxically, however, these very same characteristics have made him, together with Walter Benjamin, the most prominent Marxist who has retained the status of a classic that is still relevant in the present historical conjuncture. The American-Palestinian critic Edward Said, in his *Reflections on Exile* (2000), enumerated a series of factors that account for the enduring value of Gramsci's work, among them:

> In everything he writes Gramsci is breaking down the vulgar distinction between theory and practice in the interest of a new unity of the two. . . . The radically occasional and fragmentary

quality of Gramsci's writing is due partially to his work's situational intensity and sensitivity; it is also due to something that Gramsci wanted to preserve, his critical consciousness, which for him I think, came to mean not being coopted by a system. . . . Gramsci chose these forms [of writing] as ways of never finishing his discourse, never completing his utterance for fear that it would compromise his work by giving it the status of a text both to himself and to his readers, by turning his work into a body of *resolved* systematic ideas that would exercise their dominion over him and over his reader. (PP. 466–67)

Antonio Santucci makes a similar point, only more succinctly, when he states—in *Gramsci* (1996)—that, like every other authentic classic, Gramsci's work is an expression of its epoch, but at the same time it "resists contingency and remains open to dialogue with future generations" (p. 13). With his steadfast focus on Gramsci's writings, Santucci compels his readers to engage in an open-ended dialogue with it—he was driven by the conviction that Gramsci's legacy is truly *für ewig*.

The "Spirit of Scission"

by Lelio La Porta

This volume reproduces Antonio Santucci's *Antonio Gramsci. Guida al pensiero e agli scritti* [Antonio Gramsci: A Guide to His Thought and Writings (Editori Riuniti, 1987)] in its entirety, as well as the first chapter of *Gramsci* ["Fin de Siècle Gramsci" (Newton & Compton, Rome 1996)]. The former contributed greatly to spreading Gramsci's ideas in Italy, and the latter is one of the sharpest reflections on the fate of Gramsci's ideas after 1989. As Eric Hobsbawm writes in his Preface, the publication of this volume is a way of remembering "the most important philologist of Gramsci's texts" as well as "Gramsci's major interpreter."

The full list of Santucci's works has been published in "Antonio Santucci: Bibliography" in the newsletter of the International Gramsci Society (December 2004)[1] and in J. Cammett's *Bibliografia Gramsciana 1922–1988* (Editori Riuniti, 1991, continuously updated by the Gramsci Institute Foundation). Santucci was not only a historian of Gramsci, but also the editor of several volumes of *The Marx-Engels Letters* and

Labriola's Correspondence. In 1993, he published Diderot's *Return to Nature* (Editori Laterza). From his reading of Diderot, which highlighted the themes of anticolonialism and the damage of colonization, Santucci posed the following question: is it possible to constitute a society that can function as a meeting point between civil progress and humanity's natural roots? Santucci argued that a return to nature would certainly appear as a utopia, but the possibility of usefully appropriating Diderot's ethics (the ecology of humanity) should not be excluded.

In 1987, Santucci took part in *"Vigencia y Legado de Antonio Gramsci"* [The Power and Legacy of Antonio Gramsci], a conference organized by the Instituto de Ciencias Alejandro Lipschutz in Santiago, Chile.[2] Santucci often talked about this experience—which remarkably took place during the Pinochet dictatorship—remembering how 5,000 people defied all sorts of proscriptions to attend the conference. He was equally proud when accepting initiatives undertaken by lyceums.[3] Never too academic or pedantic, Santucci used to start from what was commonly known to his young listeners and then, with Cartesian clarity, he would address more complex topics until he finally came to the big theoretical questions.

Santucci struggled, with "passionate fervor," to guard against any reformist uses of Gramsci, while rediscovering the rarely discussed centrality of truth as a theme in the works of the Sardinian thinker. To this theme, taken as a possible path to understanding Gramsci's political vitality, Santucci devoted one of his last interventions, *Senza Comunismo* [Without Communism].[4] This is his most notable intellectual legacy. In this work, Santucci discussed all three of his main sources of inspiration—Labriola, Gramsci, and Marx. The volume includes an essay that explicitly refers to the concept of "living philology" and is dedicated to Garin and Gramsci's method. Santucci was the embodiment of "living philology." In remembering Sichirollo, he was fond of saying how he was "rigorous about books, in an old-fashioned way."[5] Not at all inclined to solicit the text for meaning, he called on everyone, beginning with the undersigned, to use accuracy and monkish patience as tools for gaining the best working and research methods.

Santucci—the man, the academic, the scholar and historian—is well represented by a passage from the *Margini* [Margins] column, in Gramsci's *La Città Futura* [The Future City], which was quoted by Santucci during a conference on Gramscian studies in Rome in 1987:[6]

> When arguing with an adversary, try to put yourself in his shoes. You will understand him better and perhaps you will end up realizing that he is a little, if not a lot, right. I followed this wise suggestion for a while, but my adversaries' clothes were so filthy that I came to the conclusion that it is better to be unjust sometimes, rather than to feel this sense of disgust that makes me faint.

The "spirit of scission" that enables each of us to "become aware of one's own historical personality," this was and is Santucci.

ANTONIO GRAMSCI

ABBREVIATIONS

AP   A. Natoli, *Antigone e il prigioniero. Tania Schucht lotta per la vita di Antonio Gramsci* [Antigone and the Prisoner: Tania Schucht's Struggle to Save Antonio Gramsci's Life], second edition, Rome, 1991.

CF   *La Città Futura 1917–1918* [The Future City 1917–1918], edited by S. Caprioglio, Turin, 1982.

CPC   *La costruzione del Partito comunista 1923–1926* [The Formation of the Communist Party 1923–1926], Turin, 1971 (1978).

CT   *Cronache torinesi 1913–1917* [Turin Chronicles 1913–1917], edited by S. Caprioglio, Turin, 1980.

D   *2000 pagine di Gramsci* [2000 Pages by Gramsci], 2 volumes, edited by N. Gallo and G. Ferrata, Milan, 1964.

FGD   P. Togliatti, *La formazione del gruppo dirigente del Partito comunista italiano nel 1923–1924* [The Formation of the Italian Communist Party Leadership in 1923–1924], Rome, 1962 (1982).

L   *Lettere 1908–1926* [Letters 1908–1926], edited by Antonio A. Santucci, Turin, 1992.

LC   *Lettere dal carcere* [Letters from Prison], 2 volumes, edited by A. A. Santucci, Palermo, 1996.

LTG   P. Sraffa, *Lettere a Tania per Gramsci* [Letters to Tania on Behalf of Gramsci], introduced and edited by V. Gerratana, Rome, 1991.

NL   *Nuove lettere di Antonio Gramsci con altre lettere di Piero Sraffa* [New Letters by Antonio Gramsci with Other Letters from Piero Sraffa], edited by A. A. Santucci, Rome, 1986.

NM   *Il nostro Marx* [Our Marx], edited by S. Caprioglio, Turin, 1984.

ON   *L'Ordine Nuovo 1919–1920* [The New Order 1919–1920], edited by V. Gerratana and A. A. Santucci, Turin, 1987.

Q   *Quaderni del carcere* [Prison Notebooks], edited by V. Gerratana, Turin, 1975.

SF   *Socialismo e fascismo. L'Ordine Nuovo 1921–1922* [Socialism and Fascism: The New Order 1921–1922], Turin, 1966 (1974).

SP   *Scritti politici 1916–1926* [Political Writings 1916–1926], 3 volumes, edited by P. Spriano, Editori Riuniti, Rome, 1973.

N.B.: Santucci's 1987 citations of the *Prison Notebooks* are from the version edited by Sergio Caprioglio and Elsa Fubini (Einaudi Editore, Turin, 1965).

Introduction

No writing can substitute the thinking mind or determine *ex
novo* intellectual and scientific interest where there is only interest for coffee-shop chatter or where one thinks of life as merely
self-amusement and having a good time.
— A N T O N I O   G R A M S C I , *Quaderno 8* [Notebook 8]

Research published at the end of 1986 revealed that Antonio
Gramsci is one of the 250 most frequently cited authors in arts
and humanities literature worldwide. This confirms what has
been well known for many years: hundreds of books and thousands of essays and articles have been written on this eminent
communist intellectual, not only in Italy but around the world.
This makes it very difficult to put together a complete bibliography of Gramscian critical approaches.

At times, the literature on some personalities or historical,
political, scientific, and artistic events becomes unwieldy.
Usually it has to do with the "classics," that is, personalities,
works, or events that continue to attract an interest far beyond
their own temporal and geographical boundaries. The fundamental characteristic of a "classic" is its universality; however,
there are other particular elements that converge to stimulate

and multiply studies and works. One such element deserves
special mention. Often one looks at a classic author from various perspectives. Maybe one approaches the classic out of some
necessity, looking for answers that seem far from the field in
which that classic is traditionally viewed. This makes for the
general widening of interest, unthinkable for what is on the contrary regarded as the exclusive object and technical patrimony
of a few specialists. Examples of this sort could be numerous,
yet very few reach the stature of Gramsci's work, especially
when considering Italian culture.

In a letter dated August 1932, Gramsci writes:

Modern man[1] should be a synthesis of those who will become . . .
hypostatized as national characteristics—the American engi-
neer, the German philosopher, the French politician—recreat-
ing, so to speak, the Italian Renaissance man, the modern version of Leonardo da Vinci, now man of the masses or collective
man, though maintaining a strong personality and individual
originality. A trifle, as you can see. (LC, p. 601)

The ironic conclusion of these lines already expresses
Gramsci's awareness of how Renaissance man constitutes an illusory model for "modern man." In a note from the *Prison
Notebooks*, one reads that "Renaissance man is no longer possible
in the modern world, whenever larger masses of humans actively
and directly participate in the making of history" (Q, p. 689).

It would be unjust to Gramsci to find the reasons for the
popularity of his works in his generic versatility, in the large
range of his intellectual interests, or in some tendency for eclec-
ticism. In Gramsci's case, the "Renaissance man" metaphor
can only be meaningful relative to the way Gramsci used it in
reference to Benedetto Croce,[2] the only Italian of the nineteenth century whose works had an equally intense and enduring influence among various intellectual classes. Gramsci's

unique abilities lay in expressing "international and cosmopolitan necessities and relations" and making national ones coincide "with civilizational linkages far larger than the national" (Q, p. 1302). It is this capacity that can introduce comparisons with those intellectuals who served, "almost collegially," a similar function in Italy from the Middle Ages to the end of the *Seicento* (seventeenth-century).

Referring to the Neapolitan philosopher Croce, Gramsci observes:

> The most important element of Croce's popularity is intrinsic to his very same thought and to his mode of thinking, and is traceable to his philosophy's greater concern for life . . . . He dismantled the conceptualization of philosophy as a "closed" and definitive system, and therefore pedantic and abstruse. He thereby affirmed that philosophy's main task must be to resolve the problems that presented themselves from time to time in the unfolding of history. Systematicity is not to be discerned in some external architectural structure, but in the inner coherence and fecund comprehensiveness of every particular solution (Q, p. 1216).

In broad terms, this assessment of Croce's popularity can be applied to Gramsci himself. It is from this observation that we should begin to understand why Gramsci's writings have been read and commented upon by historians and philosophers, literary figures and theater historians, scientists, party leaders and militants, students and teachers, who come from the most diverse ideological and political persuasions.

Parallels between the works of Gramsci and Croce are inevitable and intricate. It is true that both consider philosophy as "history of philosophy." That is, philosophy develops as the general history of the world develops, "not only because a great philosopher is succeeded by an even greater one" (Q, p. 1273).

However, from this shared premise, the two derived opposing results and perspectives.

Even from the viewpoint of simple elaboration, Croce's and Gramsci's writings reveal profound differences. In considering Italian cultural history, it is worth remembering that these two eminent scholars carried out their activities outside of academic institutions. Not only were they outsiders to academic circles, but neither of them completed regular university studies toward a degree. Despite this coincidence—which also reveals traditional limitations in the organization and politics of culture in Italy—the experiences and working conditions of Croce and Gramsci could not be further apart.

Although he was self-taught, Croce was not deprived of opportunities for scientific activity. Over a fifty year span, he published his findings regularly and in their entirety. But an utterly different situation emerges in the case of Gramsci's writings.

It is a common task of scholarship to list an author's works in chronological order. Sometimes the author himself suggests the presence of various phases inside his opus, relating them to external circumstances (historical and biographical) or to internal ones (developments, revisions, adherence to new ideas and so on). It seems obvious to point out that Gramsci's output is decisively marked by the dramatic turn in his private and intellectual life as a result of his arrest. Thus, we must distinguish between the writings preceding his incarceration and those of his prison years. To the former belong the hundreds of articles published in various periodicals until the end of 1926; to the latter belong the *Letters from Prison* and the *Prison Notebooks*.

In his *Questions of Method*, Gramsci reflects on the framework for a correct understanding of Marx's thought. He asserts that, among the works of the founder of scientific socialism, "one must distinguish between those that were brought to completion and published and those unpublished because unfinished." He continues:

It is evident that the content of these posthumous works must be read with much discretion and caution, since it cannot be considered anything but material still in its developmental stage, still provisional. . . . A work can never be identified with its crude material, gathered for its compilation. The final choice, the disposition of the component elements, and the major or minor weight given to this or that element gathered during the preparatory stage are in fact what constitutes the actual work. (Q, p. 1842)

It is plausible to think that such observations are linked to Gramsci's concerns about his own situation. More than once in the *Prison Notebooks*, Gramsci informs us that his notes "are all to be revised and thoroughly checked." Written with "a flowing pen," it is even possible that "after having been revised, they must be integrally rewritten because exactly the contrary of what is written might be correct" (Q, p. 1365). But this is not enough:

Even the study of the correspondence must be done with some caution: a statement that is crossed out in a letter might not be repeated in a book. The stylistic vivacity of letter writing is often artistically more effective than the more measured and pondered style of a book. Sometimes it brings about argumentative deficiencies. In letters, as in speech and conversation, reasoning mistakes occur more often; the greater rapidity of thought comes often at the expense of its soundness. (Q, p. 1843)

If these methodological recommendations are to be applied to the *Prison Notebooks* and the *Letters from Prison*, one could ask which work of Gramsci better reflects his true intentions. The former are a sort of fragmentary memorandum, awaiting its development. The *Letters* are private texts—some even intimate—and not intended for the public.

Thus, one resorts to his political writings, which were published under the direct authority of the author. Yet Gramsci himself warns against excessive simplification. The criteria by which one favors an edited book over unedited material are not absolute. Similarly, with the *Letters*, newspaper articles represent extemporaneous dialogue. The quotidian chase after an ever-changing reality does not allow for the solid thinking usually found in a book. In September 1931, Gramsci reminded his sister-in-law Tatiana Schucht that:

> In ten years of journalism, I have written enough lines to compose 15 or 20 volumes of 400 pp. each; however, they were written for the day and, in my view, they should have died once the day was over. I have always refused to group them into a collection, even if of limited scope. (LC, p. 457)

All of these questions regarding interpretation are worthy of careful consideration, but their weight is felt most in the philological research that remains to be completed, which is necessary for a reliable reconstruction of the body of Gramsci's works. As with every author, the task must be "detailed and conducted with the utmost scruples, scientific integrity, intellectual loyalty, and deprived of preconceptions and biases" (Q, pp. 1840–1841).

The question that remains concerns the best way to follow Gramsci's entire intellectual development. It may be appropriate to insist on accepting his suggestions:

> elements that became stable and "permanent," that is, those elements that had been assumed as one's own, different from and superior to the "material" studied before and which functioned as stimulus. . . . The search for the *leitmotif*, the rhythm of the thought progress, must be more important than individual casual statements and loose aphorisms. (Q, ibid.)

This is all the more true when one deals with a "personality whose theoretical and practical activities are indissolubly interwoven, an intellect engaged in constant creation and perpetual movement."

And he is an explicit confirmation of how the best way to understand an author who is also involved in political action is to begin from a "biographical reconstruction not only in terms of practical but *especially* of intellectual activity" (Q, p. 1841).

The best known among Gramsci's letters is the one written to Tatiana on March 19, 1927. In it, he outlines the basis of his *Notebooks*. They are organized in four themes. One is a study of the formation of the public spirit in the *Ottocento* (nineteenth century), that is, "on Italian intellectuals, their origins, their grouping according to cultural currents, different methods of thinking, and so on." Another theme deals with comparative linguistics. A third involves a study of Luigi Pirandello's theatrical works. And finally, there is a plan for an "essay on serialized fiction and popular taste in literature." The common thread among these topics is "the popular creative spirit, in its various phases and degrees of development" (LC, pp. 56–57).

Subsequently, the organization of the work is reformulated in the introductory note to Notebook 8, begun in 1931. The title is *Note sparse e appunti per una storia degli intellettuali italiani* [Notes and Scattered Musings for a History of Italian Intellectuals]. The following year, the title of Notebook 12 becomes *Appunti e note sparse per un gruppo di saggi sulla storia degli intellettuali* [Notes and Scattered Musings for a Set of Essays on the History of Intellectuals]. Thus Gramsci gradually broadens the horizon of such a history of intellectuals. First he drops the temporal limit mentioned in the 1927 letter and changes it to intellectuals in the "last century." Later, the confinement to national context is also modified. It is no longer about "Italian intellectuals," but simply about "intellectuals." Here, then, is the leitmotif permeating Gramsci's entire oeuvre, which can be understood as a general investigation of the role of intellectuals and the organization of culture.

Gramsci's attention to cultural questions was evident in his earliest studies and writings. He followed Matteo Bartoli's lectures on linguistics with particular interest. Gramsci's first critical theater reviews go back to 1915, published in the section "*Teatri*" in the Piedmontese edition of *Avanti!* There is already in the twenty-year-old journalist a deep sense for these issues and for their potential. In the January 1916 edition of *Grido del Popolo* [The People's Cry], Gramsci expressly related culture to socialism through an article purposefully entitled "*Socialismo e cultura*" [Socialism and Culture]. In it, he points out how it is the proletariat that mainly bears the brunt of the negative effects of an approach to education as encyclopedic knowledge:

> in which man is seen merely as a container to be filled and loaded with empirical data, with raw and disconnected facts that he must later assimilate in his brain like columns in a dictionary, so as to be then able to react accordingly to the various stimuli of the external world.

According to Gramsci, such cultural training (education) only serves:

> to generate misfits, people who believe themselves superior to the rest of humanity because they have amassed in their heads a certain amount of dates and data, which they rattle off at every opportunity so as almost to make a barrier between themselves and the others.

To this pedantic approach Gramsci opposes quite a different one:

> Culture is . . . organization, discipline of one's own inner self, it is ownership of one's own personality, is the attainment of a

superior conscience, through which one's own historical worth, one's role in life, one's rights and duties become understood. However, all of the above cannot occur by spontaneous evolution, by actions and reactions independent of one's will, as in vegetable and animal life, in which every single being unconsciously selects and specifies its own organs according to a pre-established order of things. Man is above all spirit, that is, historical creation; it is not nature. Otherwise, it would be difficult to explain why, the exploited and the exploiter and the creator of wealth and its egotistic consumers having always existed, socialism has not been realized yet. The fact is that only gradually—layer upon layer—has mankind become aware of its worth and has conquered the right to live independently of the planning and the rights of minorities that have asserted themselves in prior times. And this conscience has been shaped not through the brutal sting of physiological necessities, but through intelligent reflection, at first by a few and then by an entire social class, about the best methods to convert a state of vassalage into a state of rebellion and social reconstruction. This means that every revolution has been preceded by an intense critical activity, by cultural penetration, by the permeation of ideas through the gathering of individuals, recalcitrant at first and only concerned with solving their own economic and political problems, day by day, hour by hour, without bonds of solidarity with others enduring the same conditions. (CT, pp. 100–101)

The above passage contains important and formative elements of Gramsci's thought. What emerges above all is the close bond between culture and politics. Historical periods exist during which cultural activity takes shape as political activity: "the intense activity" that precedes every revolution. The French Revolution of 1789 stemmed from the Enlightenment, which had formed all over Europe "a universal conscience, an interna-

tional bourgeois spirituality sensitive in all its parts to shared suf-
ferings and misfortunes and which revealed itself to be the best
preparation for the bloody revolt that took place later in France"
(CT, pp. 101–102).

The task of the intellectuals, however, is not just to "plow"
the land for the revolution, or generally to anticipate the unfolding of history on the level of ideas. It indeed behooves men of
culture to criticize those views of the world whose progressive
function has been surpassed. However, Gramsci's definition of
an intellectual is quite a broad one. In 1931 he writes: "I do not
limit myself to the current notion which refers to great intellectuals" (LC, p. 458). On the one hand, therefore, there is the notion
of culture as the destructive criticism of dominant ideologies and
on the other, as a constructive political project, penetration, and,
cultural aggregation. "That all political party members must be
considered intellectuals is a statement that lends itself to joking
or caricature; and yet, if one thinks about it, there is nothing
more accurate" (Q, p. 1523).

Along the lines of such an articulated leitmotif, it becomes
clear how topics that are at first sight heterogeneous are an integral part of a research agenda on intellectuals: language and
folklore, the Renaissance and the Reformation, Croce's philosophy and Niccolò Machiavelli's thought, but also the analysis of
American society and the state, the theoretical and political re-
elaboration of Marxism, with the background of the October
Revolution and the experiences of the Communist
International, of the crisis of the proletarian movement and the
rise of fascism.

The basis for the popularity of Gramsci's work was already
laid down in the research agenda formulated by the author.
There are few topics and disciplines that do not appear in his
writings that are not explored more or less in depth. In the
Notebooks, there is an instance where Gramsci reflects on a well-
known maxim: "The real Babel is not so much a place where

many different languages are spoken as much as a place where everybody thinks they are speaking the same language, while giving different meanings to the same words" (Q, p. 1818). The wide range of meanings currently attributed to terms such as "culture," "intellectuals," and "politics" runs the risk of making them rather vague. It might therefore be useful to illustrate Gramsci's special sensitivity with a specific instance, in which he shows the political-cultural nexus central to his thought.

In the *Notebooks*, the name Antonio Labriola—considered by some to be the first authentic theoretician of Italian Marxism—recurs frequently. He was the author of the renowned *Essays on the Materialist Conception of History*, published at the end of the nineteenth century. Gramsci recommends the reprinting of "Labriola's philosophical position, little known outside a narrow circle" (Q, p. 1507). In terms of the public at large, one of the reasons for the limited popularity of Labriola's thought can certainly be attributed to the abstruse nature of his writings, which reflected the work of a professional philosopher. Without contrasting Labriola's and Gramsci's interpretations of Marx, which both converge and diverge on central points, it is possible to determine Gramsci's characteristic style in themes pertaining directly to the cultural realm.

In July 1928, an article entitled "*De Amicis e il suo socialismo*" [De Amicis and His Socialism] appeared in *Lo Stato operaio* [The Proletarian State], published in Paris by the exiled leadership of the *Partito Comunista d'Italia* [Communist Party of Italy]. The article was in a separate appendix to the correspondence between Labriola and Marx's chief collaborator, Friedrich Engels. The article, published in German in 1892 in the social-democratic organ *Die Neue Zeit* [The New Time], was written by the Swiss socialist Adam Maurizio. During the difficult early years of Italian socialism, the latter had mediated in the Labriola-Engels correspondence. The article on Edmondo De Amicis had been entirely inspired by Labriola, who can be considered its true author. De Amicis's "conversion to socialism," made public in 1891, had become the object of a ruthless invective. This "bourgeois philanthropist" belonged to a group very much detested by Labriola, one of whose aims was to make socialism "likable," presenting the social question more as "a matter of the heart than a question of intelligence." Gramsci also suspected that narrow-minded interest was behind the political choices of the author of the book *Cuore* [Heart]. This led him to the following conclusion:

> There is every reason today to consider De Amicis as much a monarchist, patriot, and bourgeois as before. Very likely, his conversion, because of the spicy flavor which comes with it, will save his literary career from failure. That De Amicis can be of any use to socialism, as much as it is useful to him, we are very much in doubt.

Similarly uncompromising is Gramsci's criticism of the political tendencies of another very popular Italian writer, Giovanni Pascoli. Sent to prison in 1878 as a member of the International, this poet, a native of Romagna, later came to support a romantic and nationalistic understanding of socialism.

> I consider myself a socialist, profoundly socialist—Pascoli once said—albeit a socialist of humanity, not of some class. And my socialism, as much as it embraces all peoples, I feel does not contrast with colonial desire and aspiration. Oh, how I would have preferred that a bold and young socialist party would have placed itself at the head of Italian colonization! But, alas, its theorists made it decrepit.

It is noteworthy that, by reporting this passage in *The Notebooks*, Gramsci shows an immediate preoccupation—beyond political condemnation—with seeing "in Pascoli's poetry a reflection of this concept of his and in the didactical Anthologies" (*Notebooks*, p. 206). Gramsci views the "heroic" character of Pascoli's nationalistic brand of socialism as a point of artistic disagreement. He "wished to be a poet of epics and a popular bard, even while being of a rather 'intimate' temperament." In sum, the rhetorical style of Pascoli's socialism is translated into "an ugliness of many compositions, into a false naïvety that becomes true puerility" (Q, p. 210).

In general, Gramsci devotes much more attention to cultural, rather than artistic, creations in his writings. Culture plays a decisive role in the making of men and historical subjects, and thus is an essential part of politics. Art, in contrast, possesses a margin of autonomy from politics. Writing to his companion Julia Schucht in June 1931, Gramsci observed: "I think that an intelligent and modern person must read the classics with a certain 'detachment,' that is, only for the sake of their aesthetic values" (LC, p. 425).

Up to this point, Gramsci is not far from the tenets of classical Marxism. In a comment from prison on Balzac's realism, he explicitly underlines the agreement of his point of view with that of the "founders of the philosophy of praxis," Marx and Engels (Q, p. 1699). But while the measure of an artist's political position cannot be used to measure his greatness, it is nevertheless true that criticism must always be "militant" and never "frigidly aesthetical." The type of literary criticism proper to historical materialism, in Gramsci's view, is offered by Francesco De Sanctis, "a man who takes sides, who is anchored to sound moral and political beliefs, does not conceal them, nor even tries." The critique of a work's "structure" must be turned into "a struggle for culture, that is, a new humanism, a critique of customs and feelings, a passionate fervor" (Q, p. 426). Here again, we find a clear statement on the political function of culture.

As a militant socialist and leader of the Communist Party, Gramsci contributed tremendously to the struggles and development of the Italian and international proletarian movement. It would therefore be erroneous to see him only or mainly as a great intellectual. On the contrary, it is important to clarify that Gramsci was primarily a politician who did not hesitate to criticize the behavior of thinkers who never got deeply involved in politics, behaviors that are never "genuinely political, but rather 'cultural-political' or 'intellectual-political'" (Q, p. 1499).

This volume aims to introduce Gramsci's literary work, subdivided into three distinct parts: his political writings, *Letters from Prison* and the *Prison Notebooks*.

Gramsci's human and political experiences have long been consigned to historical texts. As a matter of fact, contemporaries such as Giuseppe Prezzolini and Piero Gobetti had already defined him, since the early 1920s, as "one of the most eminent of Italian men," even as a "prophet." Regardless, Gramsci is a model that is difficult to imitate because of his ability to mesh theory and practice and his capacity for integrating thought and action. A political biography that did not take his constant theoretical research into consideration would be unthinkable. From a reading of his work there cannot but emerge the image of a man who participates profoundly in the minor and major events of his time. He was a man who wrote about himself that there are those "who think of me as a great Satan and others as almost a saint. I wish to be neither a martyr nor a hero. I think I am simply an average man, who has his profound convictions, and who does not barter them for anything in the world" (LC, pp. 117–118).

Entire generations of democrats and antifascists considered this "average man" on a par with a mythological figure. The first edition of the *Letters* gave way to elements that fueled the creation of a legend, depicting Gramsci as a revolutionary man of unshakeable faith and iron will. The recent publication of more letters from Gramsci's correspondence has returned the "true Gramsci," the man he really was, to us. He would never have accepted being viewed as the charismatic leader of the working class. In modern times, according to Gramsci, what is called "charisma" always coincides "with a primitive phase of mass parties, when doctrine is introduced to the masses as something so nebulous and incoherent that it needs an infallible pope to interpret it and adapt it to circumstances" (Q, p. 233). On another occasion, but in a sarcastic tone, Gramsci would underline the need to beware of becoming convinced that "a politician must be a great orator or a great intellectual, must be 'anointed' as a genius, etc., etc." Such a belief is close "to the backwardness of some rural regions . . . among whom one has to have a beard to be followed" (Q, p. 1302).

Gramsci's most concerned scholars have long endeavored to prevent his legacy from being turned into a sort of "Gramsciism," in the sense of an infallible dogma. Nowadays it is easier to look at Gramsci without being saddled with the mythology around him as a great historical figure. With the passage of time, passions become subdued and give way to a more fecund reflection on the work at hand. A dialogue with this revolutionary thinker is therefore still possible through his writings. More than this, it is recommended to all those who, in spite of fully living in their own present, are not satisfied with exclaiming, as the character that Gramsci amusingly recalls in the *Prison Notebooks* did: "You say I am nothing. Well, I am still something, I am a contemporary!" (Q, p. 285).

The Political Writings

1. "The freest of journalists, always of a single opinion."

In a comment in Notebook 2, titled *Introduction to the Study of Philosophy* and edited by Gramsci in 1932–1933, one reads:

> It is possible that an eminent personality expresses his most productive thoughts not in a sphere apparently most "logical" to him, according to an external classification scheme, but in another apparently alien one. When a politician writes about philosophy, maybe he expresses his "true" philosophy in his political writings instead. In every personality there is a dominant activity and a predominant one. It is in the latter that his thought must be analyzed. (Q, p. 1493)

For some years, journalism was Gramsci's dominant activity. He continued to work as a journalist until the time of his arrest, even as his duty as a political leader became predominant.

In October 1931, in a letter from Turi prison, Gramsci writes:

I was never a professional journalist, who sells his pen to those
offering more money, thereby being compelled to lie constantly
as part of the trade. I was the freest of journalists, always of a single opinion and I have never had to hide my deep convictions
just to please some boss or ruffian. (LC, p. 478)

Gramsci's statement, full of pride and moral passion, reveals a
new type of journalism, one whose aim is the building of a truly
new society. Before examining the origin of Gramsci's activity as
a journalist and how it developed into an organic expression of
his theoretical reflection and political action, it is appropriate to
place it within the context of his own literary work.

It has already been mentioned that Gramsci was against the
idea of collecting his articles into volumes because they would
have given the false appearance of an internal coherence expected
in a book, instead of preserving the provisional and contingent
characteristics of their original publication. In spite of this,
Einaudi Editore published the first complete edition of Gramsci's
works in twelve volumes, *Opere di Antonio Gramsci*, between
1947 and 1971. It included five volumes of Gramsci's political
writings. Most of them are press articles organized as follows
(publication dates in parentheses):

- *Scritti giovanili* [Youthful Writings], 1914–1918 (1958)
- *Sotto la Mole* [Under the Mole Antonelliana Monument],
  1916–1920 (1960)
- *L'Ordine Nuovo* [The New Order], 1919–1920 (1954)
- *Socialismo e fascismo. L'Ordine Nuovo* [Socialism and
  Fascism: The New Order], 1921–1922 (1966)
- *La costruzione del partito comunista* [Building the
  Communist Party], 1923–1926 (1971)

Other collections were later added to this list. Einaudi also
initiated a new edition of Gramsci's works in 1980 that would

include seven volumes of his political writings, taking into account the most recent research as far as the texts and critical methodologies are concerned.

These references can be useful tools both in the study of Gramsci's works and in determining the particular characteristics of his political writings compared to the *Letters* and the *Notebooks*. The first difference seems to stem from the fact that in republishing Gramsci's press articles in book form, one has in some way gone against the author's will. In reality, however, the letters were not meant to be made public, nor could Gramsci himself ever have imagined that his *Notebooks* would appear in print. Gathering Gramsci's political writings and making them easily accessible has in fact been a very useful initiative, yet Gramsci's reservations should not be discounted. They express a legitimate concern that must guide the reading of these texts. Neither book format nor chronological and thematic orderings should deceive us. It is still about articles "written for the day" so as to document Gramsci's political thought. Drawing general assessments and conclusions from the analysis of individual texts will more often result in erroneous interpretations. Only by studying the documents together, identifying their interconnections and interrelations, can one form a reliable picture of Gramsci's ideas and political activity. On this score, the leitmotif is once again more important than fortuitous and disjointed statements, often dictated by reasons of immediate journalistic polemic.

An important fact to consider with the political writings and other works is that while the *Notebooks* and the *Letters* can be safely attributed to Gramsci (the original manuscripts have been preserved), the same cannot be said for his articles. Most of them are anonymous and sometimes signed with a pseudonym. So, to determine Gramsci's authorship it is necessary to resort to a series of rigorous scientific criteria. The only criterion that is sufficient by itself is Gramsci's own authentication of such documents in his autobiographical writings. In other cases it is necessary to use methods such as content and stylistic analyses, comparisons with other writings, and the use of recollections and references from Gramsci's collaborators and individuals who knew him. By following the above forms of evidence and systematically reviewing the newspapers to which he contributed, it has been possible to credit Gramsci with articles previously excluded in earlier collections. The task, however, is not limited to expanding the body of his political writings. The same criteria must be used to verify the attribution of well-known articles.

There are several examples of writings included in Gramsci collections which were later attributed to other authors or whose attribution was so uncertain as to render them unreliable for analyzing Gramsci's thought. Although few such cases exist, they point to the need for very accurate philological work that is, above all, reinforced by great honesty. Gramsci's view about this matter is unequivocal. *To push the text*, that is, to make "texts say more than they really say, just for the sake of supporting a thesis" is reproachable (Q, p. 8383). However, it is even more so when forcing or eschewing every scientific criterion in order to attribute writings to an author for the purpose of validating a preconceived notion.

To maintain the integrity of Gramsci's work in its totality is not an easy task. Yet it is not necessary to engage oneself in minutely detailed research with *everything* he wrote. Every new attribution requires time-consuming work: each new finding, each unpublished document must be critically evaluated. Not everything an author writes is crucially important to the interpretation of his thought, nor is it coextensive with his "opus." Sometimes, a few lines, even an autograph, are nothing more than simple curiosities that add nothing to a broader understanding of the author. On the contrary, adding more material to existing collections of an author's writings can bring the risk of lessening the general interest in his work. Gramsci's classic work is by now the patrimony of Italian and international culture and does not deserve to be reduced to a philological dispute among specialists. Unencumbered by an indiscriminate overabundance of documentation, free from any censor's intervention, Gramsci's political writings are an exceptional testimony to an exemplary political and intellectual journey during a decisive period in Italian and labor history.

2. "I became acquainted with the working class of an industrial city."

In March 1924, Gramsci sent a letter from Vienna to his wife Julia. It is a love letter which speaks of kisses and tears, a hard life, torment, and being far away from home. With a few intense sentences, he reconstructs some fundamental moments in the development of his politics:

> Since childhood, I have been used to living in isolation and to hiding my feelings behind a mask of toughness or an ironic smile. . . . This has hurt me, for a long time. For a long time my relationships were something of enormous complexity, with every feeling multiplied or divided by seven to prevent others from knowing what I really felt. What spared me from becoming a completely lifeless rag? The rebellious instinct I felt against the rich as a young boy, because I couldn't continue to attend school, even if I had received the highest marks in all elementary school subjects, while the son of the butcher, the pharmacist, the clothing merchant could attend. This instinct extended to all the rich who oppressed Sardinian peasants and so I then thought that it was necessary to fight for the national independence of the region: "Throw the continentals to the sea!" How many times I repeated these words. Later on, I became acquainted with the working class of an industrial city and I understood the real meaning of what I had at first read from Marx out of intel-

lectual curiosity. So it is that I became impassioned with life, the
struggle, and the working class. (L, p. 271)

The industrial city mentioned by Gramsci is Turin, the city of
the automobile industry and metal workers—of the Fiat, Lancia,
Diatto, and Itala corporations. There were other culturally vibrant
industrial centers at the time. One was Milan, the capital of Filippo
Turati's reformist socialism and where futurism originated. There
was Florence, with its well-known literary publications. And there
was also Naples, which represented the fulcrum of Italian intellec-
tuality with Benedetto Croce and his *La critica* [Critique]. But it
was likely possible only in Turin to come to know the working
class fully and to become excited by its struggles.

In a report sent to the executive committee of the Communist
International in July 1920, Gramsci described the Piedmontese
capital city in these terms:

> We can say that Italy has three capital cities: Rome, the adminis-
> trative center of the bourgeois state; Milan, the national center
> for commerce and industry (all the banks, business offices, and
> financial institutions are concentrated in this city); and, finally,
> Turin, the industrial center where industrial production has
> reached the highest level of development. With the transfer of
> the capital to Rome all the intellectuals from low and middle
> bourgeois backgrounds emigrated from Turin and provided the
> newly formed bourgeois state with the administrative personnel
> necessary to its functioning. The development of big industry in
> Turin instead attracted the best of the Italian working class
> there. The development of this city is extremely interesting in
> relation to Italian history and the history of Italian proletarian
> revolution. Thus, the proletariat of Turin became the spiritual
> leader of the Italian working masses, bound to this city by mul-
> tifarious ties: family, tradition, history, and spiritual ties. Every
> Italian worker dreams of working in Turin. (*Il movimento tori-*

nese dei Consigli di Fabbrica [The Factory Councils' Turin
Movement], report sent in July 1920 to the Communist
International's Executive Committee, in ON, pp. 602–603)

Gramsci arrived in Turin in 1911, when he was twenty years
old. He went there to attend the local university and was granted
a scholarship for needy students. The impact of this large northern city marked a dramatic turn in the life of the young Sardinian.
Yet his Sardinia years would continue to affect his personality in
some respects, as well as his thought and work. Defining himself
self-critically as "three and four times provincial," Gramsci is
exceedingly severe toward himself (Q, p. 1176). With much sacrifice, he succeeded in completing secondary school and in graduating from the lyceum at Cagliari.

Gramsci's family was neither wealthy nor of humble status.
His father, a clerk, had finished lyceum and studied law for a
while. His mother's literacy can be considered exceptional, given
the very high level of illiteracy among women in small Sardinian
towns at the time. She enjoyed reading about everything and
shared this passion with her children.

Palmiro Togliatti, who at the same time as Gramsci applied
for and was granted a scholarship for his university studies in
Turin, would later recall how the strong impulse derived from
the impact with "continental" reality did not develop in a completely naïve and unprepared person:

> Antonio Gramsci was already a socialist when he came from
> Sardinia. Perhaps he was even more so because of his Sardinian
> rebellious instinct and his humanitarianism as a provincial young
> intellectual, rather than because of possessing a complete system
> of thought. This had to come from his experiences in Turin,
> through his university studies and from the working class. (P.
> Togliatti, *"Pensatore e uomo d'azione"* [Thinker and man of
> action], in *Antonio Gramsci*, Editori Riuniti, 1972, p. 69)

It was in Sardinia that Gramsci was first drawn to socialism. He began to read socialist newspapers, among which were *Avanti!* [Forward!], but he also read other publications of differing political orientations, such as Giuseppe Prezzolini's *La Voce* [The Voice], the writings of Karl Marx, and the essays and articles of Benedetto Croce and Gaetano Salvemini.

When still a student at the lyceum, Gramsci received his first press pass, and on July 26, 1910, he published his first article in *L'Unione Sarda* [The Sardinian Union], a short report from Aidomaggiore [a municipality in Sardinia]. His adherence to Marxism was then already evident. The following passage is excerpted from the concluding paragraph of his essay for his third-year Italian class at the lyceum:

> Many say that by now whatever mankind had to achieve, in matters of freedom and civilization, has already been achieved. There is nothing else to do other than enjoy the fruits of his struggles. On the contrary, I believe that there still is very much left to do. Mankind is just varnished with civilization. If merely scratched, the wolf's tough skin will appear at once. Instincts have been tamed but not vanquished, and the right of the mightiest is the only accepted one. The French Revolution eliminated many privileges and raised the oppressed many, but it did nothing more than replace one oppressing class with another. However, it left us a great teaching: privileges and social differences, being the product of societies and not nature, can be overcome. Mankind needs another bloodbath to remove many of these injustices. Let the oppressors then have no regrets for having left the masses in such a state of ignorance and savagery as they are now! (D, pp. 11, 15; also in SP, p. 55)

Some concrete signs of his future working interests—intellectual curiosity, political passion, and moral tension—were already part of Gramsci's repertoire when he went to Turin. His roots and ties to his native land, too, would be of primary importance in his mature works. In Sardinia, he had the opportunity to deepen his knowledge of a different Italy—the one of the peasants, the shepherds, the miners, and of the petit bourgeoisie of Southern Italy (the *Mezzogiorno*). Together with poverty and marginalization, he was exposed to old customs and popular folklore, which became a fertile and stimulating object of study for his research. The fruits of this lived knowledge—not a bookish one—of the "other Italy," later came to the fore in his theoretical contributions to the solution of the Southern Question, to the debates on the historical causes of the economic and social gaps that exist between the rural *Mezzogiorno* (the South) and the industrialized *Settentrione* (the North). Since his first years in Turin, Gramsci was able to oppose with strong arguments the widespread northern prejudice about the incompetence and "barbarism" of the South. This bourgeois ideology was widely accepted by the northern masses, even the proletarian ones, and the socialist party itself was spreading it. Inevitably, the misunderstanding and distrust between northern workers and their southern counterparts were to become mutual.

Gramsci engaged himself at once with the problem of overcoming this separation. He did so at first almost instinctively, then gradually with growing awareness, until the issue became central to his reflections on Italian politics and history. In his 1926 essay *Alcuni temi della quistione meridionale* [Some Issues of the Southern Question], Gramsci provides an anecdote of an event that occurred several years before the essay's publication. He recounts his eventual success in bringing about an entirely new sort of rapport between a brigade of soldiers comprised mainly of Sardinians and the socialist workers of Turin:

> The Sassari brigade took part in the repression of the August 1917 insurrectional revolt in Turin. Consequently, it was taken for granted that the brigade would never have befriended the

workers due to memories of hatred typically felt both by a population against any repression, even against the tools of repression, and by the regiments involved, on account of the soldiers that fell under the blows of the insurgents. The brigade was welcomed by a party of ladies and gentlemen offering flowers, cigars, and fruit. The soldiers' mood is portrayed by the story of a tanner from Sassari, responsible for the first propaganda survey:

> I approached a camp in X square (the Sardinian soldiers camped in squares during the first days, as if in a conquered city) and I spoke with a young peasant who cordially greeted me because he, too, was from Sassari.
> —What are you here in Turin for?
> —We are here to shoot those lords [*signori*] who are on strike.
> —But it is not the "lords" who are on strike; it is the workers and they are poor.
> —Here everybody is a lord. They all have a coat and tie, and make 30 lire per day. I know the poor in Sassari and I know how they are dressed; yes there are many poor there; we, "the ditch-diggers," are all poor and make only 1.50 per day.
> —But I am a worker, too, and I am poor.
> —You are poor because you are a Sardinian.
> —But if I strike with the others will you shoot me, too?
> The soldier pondered a little and then said, putting his hands on my shoulder:
> —Listen, when you strike with the others, stay at home!
> (CPC, pp. 143–144)

In spite of the fact that most of the soldiers shared this mood, the brigade was disbanded after a few months and sent away from Turin. It left suddenly at night, without any elegant crowd to cheer it on. Those occurrences were not without consequences:

they had reverberations that still hold good today and continue to deeply influence the masses. For a while, they enlightened minds that had never before thought in that way and so were impressed and radically changed. (CPC, p. 144)

Here, too, we can discern a significant aspect of Gramsci's method. Action and political ferment are revisited with the passing of time and are turned into an object and model of scientific inquiry.

3. Turin: The University and Political Involvement

The beginning of Gramsci's university life was very painful. He had arrived in Turin already strained by a year of serious difficulties. There is a letter from Gramsci to his younger brother Carlo from this period that is among the most dramatic of autobiographical documents. In this letter, written from prison, he tries to comfort and exhort his brother—who was going through a critical period—rather than commiserate:

You probably envied me a bit sometimes because I had the opportunity to study. But you certainly don't know how I managed to study.

The letter's date, September 12, 1927, marked twenty years since Gramsci had left his family:

I came home only twice in fourteen years, in 1920 and 1924. Now, during all these years I have never lived like a lord, far from it. I often went through very bad times and I also starved in the most literal sense.

Gramsci recounts moving to Cagliari in 1910 to his brother Gennaro's home, and about his frugal life there, in a:

small room where all the plaster had fallen off because of the humidity and there was only a small window that opened onto a kind of well, more like a latrine than a courtyard. . . . I stopped drinking the usual small amount of coffee in the morning. Then I began to postpone my lunch so late as to save supper. For about eight months I ate only once a day and, by the end of the third year of lyceum, I was very seriously undernourished.

Within a few months, in an increasingly weakened state, Gramsci frantically prepared for the exam to obtain a university scholarship:

I left Turin as if in a state of drowsiness. I had 55 lire in my pocket. For a trip in third class, I had spent 45 of the 100 lire brought from home. The Exposition was on and I had to pay 3 lire per day just for a room. I was reimbursed for a trip in second class, about eighty lire. But this was nothing to cheer about because the exams lasted for about 15 days and I had to spend about fifty lire just for lodging. I have no idea how I was able to take the exams because I fainted two or three times. I was able to get through it but then the troubles began. From home, they were about two months late in sending me the university enrollment documents and since registration was suspended, so were the monthly 70 lire from the scholarship. A janitor saved me by finding a boarding for 70 lire on credit. I was so humiliated that I wanted to ask the authorities to send me back home. Thus, I received 70 lire and spent 70 lire for very meager accommodations. And I spent the winter with no coat, wearing a light suit for spring and fall that was all right for Cagliari. Around March 1921 I was in such bad shape that I couldn't talk for some months. When speaking, I would use the wrong words. What is more, I was living right on the banks of the Dora River and the icy fog was killing me. (LC, pp. 116–117)

Despite a nervous breakdown that forced him to interrupt his studies many times and led to the suspension of his scholarship, he was heavily involved in university life. He followed with particular interest Matteo Bartoli's course on linguistics, Umberto Cosmo on Italian literature, and Annibale Pastore on theoretical philosophy. In addition, he attended courses at the School of Law. It was at a seminar on Roman rights law that he became acquainted with, and eventually befriended, Togliatti.

Gramsci's intense devotion to studying and precarious health delayed his direct contact with the socialist movement of Turin. And this was a period filled with workers' struggles, strikes, and political ferment. He nevertheless met with young militants and well-known socialist leaders in the city, like Angelo Tasca. Gramsci's first public involvement in political struggle dates back to October 1913. This is when he lent his support, from Ghilarza, to Attilio Diffenu's Group of Action and Anti-Protectionist Propaganda in Sardinia. Gramsci's support is reported in *Voce*, on October 9; he very likely became a member of the Turin section of the Italian Socialist Party shortly thereafter.

In 1914, Gramsci supported the Young Socialists' initiative to offer Gaetano Salvemini the candidacy to fill the vacant post of parliamentary representative for Turin. Salvemini rejected the proposal, which nevertheless retained major significance as a symbol of solidarity between northern workers and the peasants of Puglia. The latter had endured the defeat of their candidate during the previous elections through government violence. At this time, the war was knocking at Italy's door. Within the Socialist Party a debate raged about demands of the party leadership and parliamentary group for the "absolute neutrality" of Italy. Gramsci intervened in this debate in the weekly *Il Grido del Popolo*'s [The People's Cry] October 31 issue. He published "*Neutralità attiva e operante*" [Active and Working Neutrality], under a column entitled "*La Guerra e le opinioni dei socialisti*" [The War and the Socialists' Views]. This was his first political writing. It is a thoughtful and nonconformist text that hardly seems to have flowed out of the pen of an obscure student and recent socialist initiate. Gramsci debuted with an important declaration of principle:

> What should be the function of the *Italian* Socialist Party (note that is not that of the *proletariat* or of *socialism*, generally speaking) in the present period of *Italian* life? Because the Socialist Party to which we give our active support is also *Italian*, that is, it is a section of the Socialist International that has undertaken the task of winning the Italian nation to the International. This *immediate* task, always *topical*, confers it *special, national* characteristics that force the party to assume a specific function in Italian life, a specific responsibility. It is a potential state in the making, antagonistic to the bourgeois state. In its long-term fight against the bourgeois state and in the development of its internal dialectic, it seeks to create an apparatus for overcoming and absorbing that bourgeois state. It is *autonomous* in the development of this function, independent of the International other than in terms of the highest goal to be achieved and of the nature that this struggle must always present, that of class struggle. ("*Neutralità attiva e operante*" [Active and Working Neutrality], in CT, pp. 10–11)

Concerning traditional Marxism, Gramsci posed for the first time the "national question" as a problem that is *internal* to workers' movements and parties. The specificity of the nation, which certainly does not exclude the internationalist scope proper to Marxism, is considered as tangible historical and social reality. With additional nuances, this will become Gramsci's most notable contribution to Marxist political theory.

For his ideas in "*Neutralità attiva ed operante*," Gramsci would later be accused of "interventionism," that is, of being in support of Italy entering the war. Such an accusation seems predicated more on the unpredictable turns in Mussolini's political positions, at the time director of *Avanti!*, than on the content of

Gramsci's writing. In fact, Gramsci argues with the reformist wing of the Socialist Party, particularly with Tasca, who—in line with the official position of the PSI (Italian Socialist Party)—supported the thesis of Italy's absolute neutrality. For his part, Tasca was arguing against an article by Mussolini entitled "*Dalla neutralità assoluta alla neutralità attiva ed operante*" [From Absolute Neutrality to Active and Working Neutrality], which appeared in the organ of PSI on October 18, 1914 (Mussolini was expelled from the party on November 24, 1914). In reality, Gramsci had intended a debate on "the *modality* of this neutrality" rather than questioning the concept of neutrality per se. According to Gramsci, the formula of absolute neutrality had been very useful at first, but revolutionaries could not just rest on defensive positions. Rather, they should take an active role in history and make the bourgeoisie face their responsibilities, thereby preparing the ground for the "greatest rupture," the revolution:

> But revolutionaries, who conceive of history as a creation of their own spirit, made up of an uninterrupted series of ruptures on other active and passive social forces, and prepare the utmost of favorable conditions for the final *rupture* (revolution), must not be content with the provisional formula of "absolute neutrality." They must transform it instead into "active and working neutrality." This means giving back to the nation's life its genuine and frank character of class struggle, in that the working class, pushing those in power to assume their responsibilities ... forces them to acknowledge the failure of their purpose, since they have led the nation, for which they claim to be its only representative, to a blind alley from which they will not be able to come out if not by abandoning to their fate all those institutions directly responsible for the nation's current and saddest of conditions. (Ibid.)

On April 12, 1915, Gramsci took his last exam and left the university for good. In the fall, he resumed his contributions to

Il Grido del Popolo [Cry of the People], where he commemorated the writer and critic Renato Serra, fallen in war, with his
article *"La luce che si è spenta"* [A Light that Has Been
Extinguished], which appeared in the November 20 issue. In
December, he became editor of *Avanti!* He remembered that
decision in this manner:

> I joined *Avanti!* when the Socialist Party was at its lowest state and
> all the skillful writers had left for the woods and repudiated the
> party. I joined *Avanti!* freely, out of conviction. During the early
> days of December 1915, I was nominated for the directorship of
> the Oulx [a small village in the province of Turin] gymnasium,
> with a salary of 2,500 lire and a three-month vacation. Instead, on
> 10 December 1915, I got involved with *Avanti!* for a monthly
> salary of 90 lire, or 1,080 lire per year. I could have made another
> choice. If I chose *Avanti!* . . . I certainly have the right to maintain
> that I was moved by a profound faith and conviction. (*"Un agente
> provocatore"* [An Agent Provocateur] in *Scritti 1915–1921*
> [Writings, 1925–1921], edited by S. Caprioglio, Milan, 1976)

4. "The corrosive acid of idiocy."

In the December 16, 1915, issue of *Avanti!*, Gramsci published a
short article titled *"Pietà per la scienza del prof. Loria"* [Pity for
Professor Loria's Science] (CT, pp. 33–34). Gramsci repeatedly
dealt in harsh terms with the economist Achille Loria, a professor
at the University of Turin at the time. In Notebook 28 of 1935,
under the heading of "Lorianism," he alludes to:

> some harmful and bizarre aspects of a group of Italian intellectu-
> als' mentality and, therefore, the incoherence of national culture
> (disarticulation, absence of a systematic critical spirit, careless-
> ness in carrying out scientific activity, lack of a cultural central

point, weakness and ethical indulgence in the field of scientific-cultural activity, etc.). (Q, p. 2321)

Many well-known personalities will feature in Gramsci's gallery of "Lorianists," from Enrico Ferri to Arturo Labriola, and from Guglielmo Ferrero to Filippo Turati.

Gramsci's 1915 article on Loria—*"il pagliaccio del pensiero, il re degli zingari della scienza"* [the clown of thought, the gypsy king of science] (*Achille Loria,* in CF, p. 576)—is an ironic and prickly commentary on one of his lectures. It represents an effective model of the type of journalism Gramsci practiced intensively until 1918, and continued to practice with decreasing frequency through 1919-1920. In fact, after a few days he began drafting hundreds of such short articles for the column *Sotto la Mole* [Under the Mole Antonelliana Monument]. At first, these were printed in the Milan edition of *Avanti!* for the page dedicated to Turin news. From December 1918 onwards, his column appeared in the Piedmontese edition of the Socialist Party organ. They consist of quick and incisive interventions, usually based on a news item, a local event, or a personality's behavior. With an original and elegant style, atypical of contemporary Italian journalism, Gramsci became involved in a firm polemic against political immorality, nationalist rhetoric, opportunism, dishonesty, and intellectual arrogance: "I like to be the corrosive acid of idiocy," he states in 1917 (*"Qualche cosa"* [Something], in CF, p. 306).

During these years, his publishing activity is not limited to commentaries in *Sotto la Mole.* He is also active as a theater critic informing *Avanti!*'s readers about performances in Turin. With a few cursive lines, with the simple style of one who is aware of addressing a largely proletarian public, Gramsci succeeds in instilling his theater reviews with far greater cultural implications. He uses the plays staged in city theaters as a pretext for highlighting the crisis of bourgeois values and relationships. Plays by such authors as Henrik Ibsen and Luigi Pirandello are not only scrutinized for aesthetic content, but also for the social contradictions that they express. "The importance of Pirandello," he later wrote in the *Notebooks*, "seems more to be of an intellectual and moral nature, that is, more cultural than artistic" (Q, p. 705).

Meanwhile, he continues to contribute to *Grido del popolo* [The People's Cry] and to give lectures in workers' circles on Marx, the French writer Romain Rolland, the Paris Commune, the French Revolution, and the emancipation of women.

Following an initiative by the Piedmontese socialist youth federation, a decision is made to publish a single propaganda issue, "*La Città futura*" [The Future City]. Gramsci asks for, and receives, sole editorship of the issue. The four-page issue appeared on February 11, 1917. Gramsci's overall theoretical and political positions, stemming from his early experience as a militant socialist, are summarized in these writings, under the titles "*Tre principii, tre ordini*" [Three Principles, Three Orders], "*Indifferenti*" [The Indifferent], and "*Margini*" [Margins]. His intellectual proclivity is reflected in the selection of other writers' texts published in *La Città futura*: "*Cos'è la cultura*" [What Is Culture?] by Gaetano Salvemini; "*Cos'è la vita*" [What Is Life?] by Armando Carlini; and "*La religione*" [Religion] by Benedetto Croce, whom Gramsci identified as "the greatest European thinker of our times" ("*Due inviti alla meditazione*" [Two Invitations to Meditation], in CF, p. 21).

What should be socialists' attitude concerning the two terms that most frequently recur in political discussions, those of *order* and *disorder*? Order is presented to citizens as something harmonious and stable. Beyond order, the "most foolish common sense" sees nothing other than uncertainty. "One does not see a new possible order, better organized than the old one," but only a "violent break." Thus, we end up going backward, "afraid of losing everything, of facing chaos and inescapable disorder" ("*Tre principii, tre ordini*," in CF, p. 5):

Socialists must not replace order with order. They must establish order in itself. The legal maxim that they want to realize is *to
make the complete realization of one's own human personality
possible for all citizens*. By putting this maxim into practice, all
established privileges cease to exist. This leads to maximum
freedom with minimum coercion. The socialist program is a
concrete universal, and can be realized by the will. It is the principle of order, of socialist order, that order which we believe will
be realized in Italy before all other countries. (ibid., p. 11)

The principle of will as revolutionary impulse leads Gramsci
to urge socialist youth to become politically involved in a coherent and disciplined manner:

I hate the indifferent, also because I am annoyed by their whining
as eternal innocents. I ask each of them how he carries out the
role that life ordained him and daily imposes on him, what he has
and especially has not done. And I feel like I can be relentless and
not have to waste my pity, nor share my tears with them . . . . I live,
I am a partisan. Therefore I hate whoever does not take sides. I
hate the indifferent. ("*Indifferenti*," in CF, pp. 14–15)

Against improvisation and dilettantism, against "provocateur"
intellectuals, "little souls always in search of a secure anchor,
throwing themselves at the first idea that promises to become an
ideal," Gramsci insists:

Men always search outside of themselves to find reasons for their
spiritual failure; they do not want to accept the fact that its cause
is only and always will be their little soul, their lack of character
and intelligence. There are amateurs of faith, just as there are
amateurs of knowledge. . . . For many, a crisis of conscience is
nothing but an expired bank draft or the desire of opening a
checking account. (*Margini* [Margins], in CF, p. 14)

Gramsci's polemic, however, is not dictated by a generic moralism. Its targets are clearly specified in the reformist tradition of Italian socialism and the doctrine to which it subscribed from the start. Socialists like Filippo Turati and Claudio Treves were convinced that the era of revolutionary strategy had passed. The right path for Italian socialism was parliamentary action, destined to improve workers' economic and social condition through gradual evolution. Such a political trend was connected to positivism, a school of thought that came to prominence in the nineteenth century. It was a belief in the absolute value of science and for the general social well-being that scientific progress would have evenutally brought about. The myth of positivist philosophy, "blind faith in all that was associated with the term 'scientific,'" is not much of a scientific idea in Gramsci's view. It is "only a mechanistic idea, a barren mechanistic one" (ibid., p. 25). Socialism was not dead. What died was the fatalism that thought of its realization as a regular natural process. Such a historical phase in theorizing socialism had definitely passed. "*The tenacious will of man* has replaced *natural law*, the preordained order of things of the pseudo-scientists" (ibid., p. 26). We now need to "hasten the future," that is, to expand this will to all the men needed to make such a will productive. This "quantitative progress," however, can be substituted by a "qualitative one," by making this will "so intense in the current minority so as to increase its influence a million-fold" (ibid., p. 28).

The often-distorted news of the events in Russia began filtering into Italy. On March 18, 1917, there was news of the Czar's overthrow. On April 29, Gramsci writes in his "*Note sulla rivoluzione russa*" [Notes on the Russian Revolution]:

> We know that the revolution was carried out by the proletariat (workers and soldiers) . . . . But is it enough for a revolution to be carried out by the proletariat for it to be a proletarian revolu-

tion? The war, too, is made by proletarians, but it is not for this reason a proletarian deed. . . . Yet we are convinced that the Russian Revolution, besides being an event, is a proletarian action and as such it must naturally develop into a socialist regime. (*"Note sulla rivoluzione russa,"* in CF, p. 138)

On August 23, 1917, a violent rebellion erupts among Turin's workers. The disappearance of bread from retailers and an intense surge of anti-war propaganda generates an insurrection. Dozens die and hundreds are wounded. A wave of arrests of socialist activists ensues, leading to Gramsci becoming secretary of the provisional executive committee of the Turin section, as well as the effective chief editor of *Il Grido del popolo*. Under such double duty, Gramsci takes part in a secret meeting of the party's extreme left in Florence, "the intransigent revolutionaries." There, he meets Amadeo Bordiga, a young socialist leader from Naples with whom he shares total opposition to the war.

On December 24, an important editorial by Gramsci appears in *Avanti!*, *"La rivoluzione contro il 'Capitale'"* [The Revolution Against "Capital"]. This article had not appeared in the December 1 issue of *Grido del popolo* due to censorship. Here, the author holds that Marx's celebrated work, *Capital*, had in fact been:

more a book of the bourgeois than of proletarians, in Russia. It was a critical demonstration of the necessity in Russia first to form a bourgeoisie prior to bringing about a capitalist era and establishing a Western type of civilization, before the proletariat could even think about revolt, class-based claims, or revolution. . . . The Bolsheviks disown Karl Marx. They show, with their examples of explicated actions and realized gains, that the canons of historical materialism are not as rigid as might be or has ever been thought. (*"La rivoluzione contro il 'Capitale,'"* in CF, p. 513)

How are we to understand Gramsci's assertion that the Bolsheviks are not "Marxists"? Of course, Engels also sometimes recalled that Marx himself had famously declared: "I am not a Marxist!" And certainly, Gramsci aims, above all, to argue against all those who made of Marx's doctrine a canon "of dogmatic and irrefutable statements." But there is more. Here, it is not just about the debate over determinism and mechanism, codified in the Marxism of the Second International that was founded in Paris in 1889. Nor is it about the simple purpose of shaking the Italian workers' movement out of its prolonged phase of theoretical and political inertia. In "*La rivoluzione contro il 'Capitale*,'" Gramsci expresses his disagreement with historical materialism, which he views as having been refuted by the events of the Russian October.

Marx explained historical movement—the succession of periods of dominance by a class over another—on the basis of an objective law. The relations within which humans live and labor are defined as "relations of production." The instruments made to confront nature, the forms of work, the necessary knowledge for improving the means of work, are defined as the "productive forces." The movement of history tends to establish a correspondence between the relations of production and the level of development of the productive forces. Finally, it is the relations of production that must adjust themselves to the development of productive forces. In his preface to *A Contribution to the Critique of Political Economy* (1859), Marx writes:

> In the social production of their existence, men inevitably enter into definite relations which are *independent of their will*,[1] namely relations of production appropriate to a given stage in the development of their material forces of production. The totality of these relations of production constitutes the economic structure of society, the real foundation, on which arises a legal and political superstructure and to which correspond definite forms of social consciousness. The mode of production of mate-

rial life conditions the general process of social, political and intellectual life. It is not the consciousness of men that determines their existence, but their social existence that determines their consciousness. At a certain stage of development, the material productive forces of society come into conflict with the existing relations of production or—this merely expresses the same thing in legal terms—with the property relations within the framework of which they have operated hitherto. From forms of development of the productive forces these relations turn into their fetters. Then begins an era of social revolution. The changes in the economic foundation lead sooner or later to the transformation of the whole immense superstructure.[2]

Even while pointing out in *Capital* that, during the course of a historical process, a society can "shorten and lessen the birth-pangs," Marx stresses that "it can neither clear by bold leaps, nor remove by legal enactments, the obstacles offered by the successive phases of its normal development" (Marx, 1867).[3]

According to Gramsci, "positivistic and naturalistic incrustations" were already present in Marx's thought. It maintains its vitality if intended as a "continuation of Italian and German idealism." Yet it is from those "incrustations" that a fatalistic interpretation of the historical process originated, which spurs the political uncertainties and hesitations against which Gramsci struggles. For the laws of historical materialism he substitutes the *subjective* element of the will, the "shaper of objective reality" ("*La rivoluzione contro il 'Capitale*,'" in CF, p. 514).

The young Gramsci's idealistic formation is also evident in other writings of this period. He is influenced by Giovanni Gentile, in addition to Hegel and Croce. Replying to accusations of "voluntarism" as a result of his "*La rivoluzione contro il 'Capitale*,'" Gramsci stated that the new generation intends to return to "Marx's genuine doctrine." However, in it "man and reality, the instrument of labor, and the will are not separate, but are connected through the *historical act*" ("*La critica critica*" [Critical Critique], in CF, pp. 555–556). This was not the only case in which Gramsci appropriates concepts and terminology from Gentile's philosophy. Moreover, in the February 9 issue of *Il Grido del popolo*, Gentile is mentioned as "the most prolific Italian philosopher in the field of thought" and a major interpreter of Marx ("*Il socialismo e la filosofia attuale*" [Socialism and Current Philosophy], in CF, p. 650).

On May 4, 1918, Gramsci writes "*Il nostro Marx*" to celebrate the centenary of the birth of the founder of scientific socialism. "Marx means the coming of intelligence in the history of humanity, the kingdom of awareness" ("*Il nostro Marx*," in NM, p. 3).

In October, the publication of *Il Grido del Popolo* comes to an end. In his farewell message to his readers, Gramsci writes:

> The socialist section of Turin, the proletarians of this province and those of Piedmont must now direct all their efforts and dedicate all their financial power to the Turin edition of *Avanti!* The editor who, from August 1917 to the present, devoted most of his time and his often feverish activity to *Il Grido*, must now be completely absorbed by working for the Turin *Avanti!* ("*Il Grido del Popolo*," in NM, p. 340)

The first issue of the Turin edition of the socialist daily paper appeared on December 5, 1917. With Gramsci and Togliatti as editors, among others, the circulation of *Avanti!* rose from 16,000 to 50,000 in a few months.

5. "Organize because we will need all our strength."

On the last page of "*La Città future*" [The Future City], Gramsci informs his readers that, with some friends, before the war, "a decision was made to start a new publication on socialist life."

The crisis during those critical years had led to the project's post-ponement. "The parts of our soul torn by the war will return to the hearth and the publication will continue" ("*La Città futura*," in CT, p. 34). The first issue of *Ordine Nuovo, Rassegna setti-manale di cultura socialista* [The New Order, Weekly Review of Socialist Culture] appears on May 1, 1919. On the left side, under the weekly's title, there is an appeal of clear Gramscian inspiration: "Educate yourselves because we will need all your intelligence. Be excited because we will need all your enthusiasm. Organize because we will need all your strength."

Much has been said and written about the cultural and politi-cal significance of *Ordine Nuovo*, about the unique place it occu-pies among Italian publications of the twentieth century. But the most interesting interpretation of, and reflection on, this "phe-nomenon" can only come from its main author, Antonio Gramsci:

> When in April 1919 the three, four, or five of us decided . . . to start the publication of this review, *Ordine Nuovo*, none of us (nobody, perhaps . . .) thought of changing the face of the world, of renewing the brains and hearts of the human multitudes, of opening a new cycle in history. None of us (perhaps, nobody— someone dreamt of 6,000 subscribers within a few months) toyed with rosy illusions on a good outcome for this enterprise. Who were we? Whom did we represent? Of what new message were we the bearers? Alas! The only feeling that united us during those meetings was one moved by a vague passion for a vague proletarian culture; we wanted to do, do, do; we felt anguished, without a sense of direction, immersed in the ardent life of those months following the armistice, when the cataclysm of Italian society appeared immediate. ("*Il programma dell'Ordine Nuovo*" [The Program of The New Order], in ON, p. 619)

In the above passage, printed August 4, 1920, Gramsci expresses even more negative judgments on the beginnings of his experience with *Ordine Nuovo*. In fact, the first issue lacked "a concrete program" and a "central *idea*" (ibid., p. 620). This was until the plotting of an "editorial *coup d'état*," together with Togliatti and with the consent of Umberto Terracini. In the seventh issue of *Ordine Nuovo*, June 21, 1919, the editorial "*Democrazia operaia*" [Workers' Democracy] appeared. In it, the problem of internal factory commissions was explicitly addressed. These were intended as future organs of proletarian power, within a system of workers' democracy similar to the one that had been developing in the Soviet Union. Hence "the *idea* of *Ordine Nuovo*," of the "fundamental problem of workers' revolution" and of "proletarian freedom":

> To us and to our followers, *Ordine Nuovo* became "the newspaper of the Factory Councils." Workers loved *Ordine Nuovo* (we can affirm this with innermost satisfaction). And why did the workers love *Ordine Nuovo*? Because in its articles they found part of themselves, the better one. . . . Because these articles were not cold, intellectual architecture, but were the outcome of our discussions with the best workers. They articulated the real feelings, will, and passion of the working class of Turin. (Ibid., p. 622)

Sidestepping Tasca's opposition to using *Ordine Nuovo* for direct propaganda among the working masses, Gramsci established *Democrazia Operaia* with Togliatti to discuss factory councils. These worker organizations were inspired by the Russian *soviets*. However, rather than trying to transpose a foreign system onto Italy, Gramsci was trying to determine whether something comparable to the soviets existed in Italian factories, particularly those in Turin, which could serve as the "seed" for a workers' government. The answer to such a question was in the affirmative: "The Socialist State is already a potential reality in the social institutions typical of the exploited working class." Socialist circles, peasant communities, especially shop-floor internal committees, are "centers of proletarian life" that must be linked, coordi-nated, and centralized. The purpose was to create a workers' democracy to counter the bourgeois state, *starting immediately*. This was so as "to take over the bourgeois state in all its essential functions of administration and of control over national wealth" (*Democrazia Operaia*, in ON, p. 87).

Internal committees were elected only by unionized workers, and since only part of the working class was represented by pro-fessional trade unions and the Socialist Party, Gramsci proposed that the opportunity to vote for the councils be extended to all workers. This included factory workers, peasants, office clerks, and technicians, even if they were not socialist. In short, all those active in the production process were to vote for their own dem-ocratic organizations, i.e., the councils. Furthermore, the latter's function had to be much farther-reaching and complex than that of the trade union. Its role was not to be limited to wage bargain-ing and the protection of workers' rights in the workplace. The councils' objective was far more ambitious. It was to take control of the entire production process. To the motto "All the shop-floor's power to the shop-floor's committees" another had to be added: "All the power of the state to the workers' and peasants' councils" (ibid., p. 89).

> The formula of "proletarian dictatorship" must cease to be only a formula, or an opportunity to show off some revolutionary phraseology. Whoever wants the ends must also want the means. Proletarian dictatorship means the establishment of a new state, a typically proletarian one, in which the institutional experi-ences of the oppressed working class come together and the social life of workers and peasants becomes a predominant and strongly organized system. (ibid., in ON, p. 90)

It has been said that in the maxim accompanying *Ordine Nuovo*, "Educate yourselves because we will need all your intelligence," was placed at the very beginning of the publication's title. Even as propaganda and political debate stiffened, *Ordine Nuovo* did not shy away from fostering cultural education and "intellectual reform."

Since December 1917, Gramsci had proposed the founding of a proletarian cultural association in Turin. Eventually, with other young people, he founded a "club of moral life." In an article published in *Grido del popolo* on December 18, titled "*Per un'associazione di coltura*" [For a Cultural Association], he states:

> One of the most serious weaknesses in our activity is this: we wait until problems arise before discussing them and decide about the direction of our line of action. Compelled by urgency, we come to hasty solutions to problems, in the sense that not all who are part of the movement have a full grasp of the situation and, therefore, if they follow an agreed-upon directive, they do so out of a sense of discipline and trust in the leadership, more than intimate conviction and rational spontaneity. ("*Per un'associazione di coltura*," in CF, p. 498)

As the above paragraph suggests, Gramsci followed the Russian revolutionary process not only in its political, economic, and social forms but also explored problems related to "cultural revolution." On June 1, 1918, he published an article by Anatoly Lunacharsky, the first Public Education Minister of the Soviet Republic, under the title of "*La cultura nel movimento socialista*" [Culture in the Socialist Movement]. In this article, Lunacharsky stated that along with the three basic practices in workers' movements—political, economic, and cooperative—a "fourth one must be recognized, on par with the others, that is, the cultural practices of proletarian self-education and creativity." In his introduction, Gramsci noted how Lunacarsky's formulation corresponded with the one supported by the *Avanti!* editorial staff of Turin:

This coincidence of thought and practical proposition is essentially and without a doubt due to the great similarity that exists between the intellectual and moral conditions of the two proletariats, the Russian and the Italian. (*La cultura del movimento socialista* [Socialist Movement Culture], in NM, p. 77)

Ordine Nuovo introduced its readers to such artists and intellectuals as Lunacharsky, Gorky, Romain Rolland, Henry Barbusse, Max Eastman, and Walt Whitman, in addition to the political writings of Lenin, Bukharin, Zinoviev, and the Hungarian Béla Kun, among others. Its purpose was not purely literary. The younger members of *Ordine Nuovo* were actually trying to build their own cultural program, one that was international in scope. They aimed to gain a place alongside the Russian movement of proletarian culture, the *"Proletkult."*

In May, Gramsci was elected member of the executive committee of the Turin socialist section and in July 1919 joined a solidarity strike in support of the communist republics of Russia and Hungary. He was arrested and jailed for a few days.

On September 13, *Ordine Nuovo* published the manifesto *"Ai commissari di reparto delle officine Fiat Centro e Brevetti"* [To the Section Superintendents of the Shops of Fiat Central and Patent Office]. With the appointment of superintendents, shop-floor internal committees acquired a new organizational form.

The workforce in other factories of the city and province followed suit. The movement, to which "our publication [*Ordine Nuovo*] gave quite a significant contribution," began to attract increasing interest. Industrialists started to ask themselves "what is its purpose, what plans does the Turin working class intend to realize?" (*Ai commissari di reparto delle officine Fiat Centro e Brevetti*, in ON, p. 208).

On October 5–8, 1919, in Bologna, the Socialist Party congress was held. It would lead to the decision of the party to join the Communist International.

A discussion ensued in political and trade union organizations about the formation of factory councils through the election of section superintendents. On November 1st, it was approved by the metalworkers' assembly of Turin, and on November 6 by the socialist section. Even the special congress of the chamber of labor approved an agenda in favor of the formation of factory councils, which were the object of very lively debates among different socialist currents.

In the January 24–31, 1920, issue of *Ordine Nuovo*, Gramsci publishes "*Programma d' azione della sezione socialista torinese*" [Action Plan of the Socialist Section of Turin]. His polemic against bureaucratic and reformist tendencies in the Socialist Party increases:

> During this last period of national and international politics we have not proven ourselves capable of giving a definite and clear direction to the class struggle fought by Italian workers. The party's activity was confused with that of the parliamentary group. That is, it was either a quite reformist and opportunistic action or an action absolutely devoid of any real educational content value, in the revolutionary meaning suggested by the Congress of Bologna, for inciting the largest number of people to support the cause and the program of the proletarian revolution. ("*Programma d'azione della sezione socialista torinese*," in ON, p. 399)

The "chaos" and "disorientation" into which the masses had fallen had to be overcome by "putting into practice the theories of the Third International, acclaimed in Bologna by a large majority and readily forgotten because of the attraction of Parliament."

In Gramsci's view, the Turin section was supposed to charge itself with pressing the party to promote the formation of the workers and peasants councils throughout the peninsula. All forms of collaboration with industrialists and the bourgeois state were to be undermined. "The solution to the nagging problems of the present can only be found through purely proletarian power, through the workers' state" (ibid., in ON, p. 400). The motto "All power to the Soviets!" had to be given real and immediate meaning.

In the *Ordine Nuovo* of March 27, an appeal entitled "*Il congresso dei Consigli di fabbrica*" [The Congress of Factory Councils] was published. It was directed to the Turin workers— as well as to all the workers of Italy—and to the peasants, their "natural allies." The reason for soliciting all workers' representatives to go to the Piedmontese capital to participate in the congress is explained as follows:

> The Turin workforce is convinced that if they happen to be the vanguard of the movement, whose purpose is to implement institutions suitable for future communist management of factory and society, it is not as much for their special worth as the fact that they found themselves under special living and working conditions that favored the development in the working masses of a revolutionary conscience and a rebuilding capacity. However, industrial centralization and the unitary discipline established in Turin industry are conditions that tend to spread to the entire world of the bourgeois economy. They are the conditions to which the dominant class looks for its own salvation.

By then, it was common knowledge that the activity of the section managers and the councils was the "preparation for the communist revolution of society." The workers had to be alert to the fact that the masters "are on notice, they are coming to an agreement to coordinate their actions so as to fight you when they deem appropriate."

The following day in Turin, the metalworks lockout was announced. The employers' offensive was a response to the so-called "strike of the hands." Daylight Saving Time had been introduced in Italy, but the industrial mechanics' section superintendents fought to keep the work schedule according to standard time. As a result of the union dispute, the whole internal committee was sacked. A strike in solidarity with the dismissed workers followed, and then all the metallurgical factories in Turin were occupied.

As a condition for returning to work, the industrialists asked for the end of the councils movement. However, the workers firmly defended their new factory institutions and reacted with a month's strike. From April 13 to 24, there was a general abstention from work; more than 200,000 Turin workers joined the strike. The *Ordine Nuovo* group backed the workers' struggle, which failed to reach the national scale. The strike ended with a substantial victory for the industrialists; most of the gains of the councils movement were suddenly wiped out. In *"La forza della rivoluzione"* [The Power of Revolution], in *Ordine Nuovo* of May 8, Gramsci would recall the atmosphere of those days in a highly evocative tone. The state had supported the industrialists with thousands of fully-armed soldiers. Agents provocateurs, "strike breakers," and bribed journalists were spreading panic and false news:

> The working class could only counter with the strikers' half-page bulletin and their energies of resistance and sacrifice. Without a wage, the metalworkers held out for a month: many suffered from hunger, had to take their furniture to the pawnshop, even mattresses and sheets; the other portion of the working population, too, endured hardship, misery, and desolation. The city was as if under siege, the working population had to endure all the ills and discomfort of a cruel and relentless siege. The strike ended in defeat. The ideal that sustained the workers was mocked even by part of the workers' representatives; the energy and faith of the leaders of the strike came to be considered wishful thinking, ingenuousness, and a mistake, even by some of the workers' representatives. (*"La forza della rivoluzione,"* in ON, pp. 518–519)

A few lines of encouragement to the workers who, in spite of everything, "did not lose confidence in the future of the working class, and in the communist revolution," are not enough to hide the political knot evinced by the April defeat. There had been no support for the Turin movement from the general Confederation of Labor and the Socialist leadership. In the same issue of *Ordine Nuovo*, the editors therefore reprinted the nine points in Gramsci's motion *"Per un rinnovamento del Partito socialista"* [For a Renewal of the Socialist Party], which had been already approved at the national meeting of the PSI held in Milan from April 18 to 23.

In Gramsci's analysis of this phase of the Italian class struggle, there are premonitory signs about the next reactionary offensive which brought fascism to power. The economic and social crises that had paralyzed the country needed to be resolved with the conquest of political power by the revolutionary proletariat. Otherwise, a terrible attack from the industrialists and the government was to be inevitable. In the second case:

> Every type of violence will be used against the industrial and agricultural proletariat to subjugate them to a state of servitude; there will be relentless attempts to break up workers' political organizations (the Socialist Party) and to incorporate organized economic resistance (trade unions and cooperatives) into the bourgeois state's machinery. (*"Per un rinnovamento del Partito socialista,"* in ON, p. 511)

At this point, Gramsci did not leave any doubt about alternatives for the Socialist Party: "From a petit-bourgeois parliamentary party it must become the party of the revolutionary proletariat." Wavering and hesitation would no longer be tolerated. The situation required the party to be "homogeneous, cohesive, with its own doctrine, its own strategy, and a rigid and implacable [internal] discipline." Finally, anyone not identifying with revolutionary communism had to be expelled. All energy had to be turned toward organizing "the workers' forces as on a warpath" (ibid., in ON, p. 515).

In the June 5th issue of *Ordine Nuovo*, Gramsci underscored the validity of the councils' project with "*Il Consiglio di fabbrica*" [The Factory Council]:

> The true process of proletarian revolution cannot be identified in the development and actions of voluntaristic and contractualistic revolutionary organizations, such as the political party and the professional trade unionists. . . . [It] is carried out in the field of production, in the factory, where relationships are between the oppressor and the oppressed, exploiter and exploited, where there is no freedom for the worker, no democracy. The revolutionary process comes about where the worker is nothing and wants to become everything, where the owner's power is unlimited, the power over the life and death of the worker, his wife, and his children. ("*Il Consiglio di fabbrica*," in ON, pp. 532–533)

Nevertheless, the lessons of April could not be ignored. Without a general direction, the movement risked stagnation or annihilation. The pressing problem of the party's identity had to be faced with maximum resolve. How could the PSI lead a truly revolutionary process while being blocked by the internal games of maximalist and reformist factions? For a long time now the group headed by Bordiga had supported the complete restructuring of the party as a priority, even at the risk of a split. But to Gramsci such a question still appeared too limited. Workers' democracy, education, and communist propaganda among the masses remained his central themes for action. But the time was ripe for a rapprochement between Gramsci and Bordiga's group and new events would contribute to hasten it.

6. The birth of the Italian Communist Party (PCI)

The Second Congress of the Communist International was held in Moscow on July 19, 1920. No one from the *Ordine Nuovo* group was part of the delegation of the Italian Socialist Party. Its members were, among others, Bordiga, leader of the "abstention-ist" faction and an opponent of parliamentary and electoral poli-tics. Another was the "electionist" Giacinto Menotti Serrati. Though differing on the issue of parliamentarism, they were both hostile to the Turin communists' political line. Yet it is Gramsci and the exponents of *Ordine Nuovo* who would gain great pres-tige during the course of the Congress.

In Italy, the councils' movement had been confined to the Turin workers' stronghold, but news of its battles and of the polit-ical project articulated in Gramsci's writings had managed to reach Lenin. Through an official of the International sent to Italy at the time, Lenin had the opportunity to read Gramsci's motion *"Per un rinnovamento del Partito Socialista"* [For a Renewal of the Socialist Party], published in *Ordine Nuovo*. Thus, in "Theses on the Fundamental Tasks of the Second Congress of the Communist International," he states that Gramsci's proposals "are fully in keeping with the fundamental principles of the Third International."

In his July 30 session reply to Serrati, who declared that he favored a gradual purge of the PSI's reformist wing but was against scission, Lenin underlines that:

> We must simply tell the Italian comrades that it is the line of *L'Ordine Nuovo* members that corresponds to the line of the Communist International, and not that of the present majority of the Socialist Party's leaders and their parliamentary group. . . . That is why we must say to the Italian comrades and all parties that have a right wing: this reformist tendency has nothing in common with communism.[4]

Bordiga's "abstentionism" was not spared Lenin's trenchant criticism either. The claim that any parliamentary participation in a bourgeois state is dangerous was wrong. The "destruction of parliament" must pass through the struggle carried out *in* parliament. "For now," Lenin concludes, "the parliament, too, is an arena for the class struggle."[5]

In the August 21 issue of *"Cronache dell'Ordine Nuovo"* [Chronicles of *Ordine Nuovo*], Gramsci remarks:

> In remembering the passionate days of last April, we are pleased, as undoubtedly are all the section's comrades and all the workers, to know that the opinion of the executive committee of the Third International is very different from the one of the major Italian exponents of the party, which seemed irrevocable; [we are pleased] to be informed that the very same opinion of the "four hotheads" of Turin was supported by the highest authority of the international workers' movement. (*"Cronache dell'Ordine Nuovo,"* in ON, p. 630)

While some of the most prominent Italian socialist leaders were still in Russia, there began a struggle in Italy that would mark the definitive defeat of the attempted revolution of 1919–1920. This time, too, it was the industrialists' intransigence that resulted in the eruption of workers' rebellion. Their refusal to meet the wage increase requested by the metalworkers' trade unions had led to the occupation of all the factories of this sector in the whole peninsula. For a month, more than half a million workers, armed as much as possible, took over factories while trying to maintain production. In Turin, the councils took over the management of work in the factory. In Lombardy, Liguria, Tuscany, and Emilia, but also in some southern towns, workers followed the example of the Piedmontese capital in trying to establish autonomous self-management.

Gramsci's hypothesis seemed at last to be vindicated by the facts. Yet in the September 2 edition of *Avanti!* he published an editorial in a pessimistic tone: "The relative ease with which the occupation of the factories was achieved should be highly pondered by the workers. They must not deceive themselves in this regard." The easy takeover, he continues, "whether it *points* to the level of weakness of capitalism or the proletariat's level of power, does not reveal in itself any new definite position. The power still remains under capital's control" (*"L'occupazione"* [The Occupation], in ON, pp. 646–647).

And Gramsci was not wrong. With the passing of days, the industrialists' front remained compact, while the workers' fragmented and were affected by strong internal rifts. Again, the movement paid dearly for a lack of centralized direction. First, there had not been complete participation in the unrest. Large numbers of proletarians were confused and remained aloof. The trade union had aimed solely at ending the dispute through government arbitration. The weight of the revolutionary minority was not sufficient to impose a radical change of direction in the socialist leadership. Among the workers, the impatience and extremism of some factions gave rise to internal disputes and divisions. The revolution was practically put to the ballot and rejected by the General Council of the Confederation of Labor.

With a compromise sanctioned by Prime Minister Giolitti, the occupation of the factories came to an end and the councils were again defeated. By the beginning of October 1920, workers everywhere went back to work.

Just as in the preceding year's April events, *Ordine Nuovo* had suspended publication during the factory occupations. Thus, a month later, on September 4 and October 9, Gramsci published two articles entitled *"Il Partito comunista"* [The Communist Party], where he undertakes an analysis of the Italian political situation and the tasks of the workers' party.

Even at the height of the metalworkers' struggle, Gramsci did not indulge in any "workerist" rhetoric. Rather, he viewed the worker as: "intellectually lazy, he does not know and does not want to see beyond the immediate, and so he lacks any criterion when choosing his leaders and lets himself be easily deceived by promises; he wants to believe he can get what he wants without great effort and without having to think too much." This was a harsh call to reality. Without abandoning his general viewpoint, the councils' theoretician did not give in to the easy demagogy of the moment. The worker can find his freedom only in the communist party, "where he can think, look beyond, and has a responsibility, where he both organizes and is organized, where he feels part of a vanguard that pushes forward, carrying the multitude with it" ("*Il Partito comunista*," in ON, p. 655).

The contemporary internal and international political phase places at the forefront the problem of the formation of the communist party. The traditional party of Italian workers, the PSI:

> did not escape the process of disintegration of all associative forms, a process characteristic of the period we are going through. It is an agglomeration of parties; it moves and cannot but move lazily and slowly; it is constantly exposed to the risk of becoming easy prey for adventurers, careerists, and ambitious people without political seriousness or ability; because of its heterogeneity, the innumerable frictions in its gears, worn out and sabotaged by servant-masters, it is never capable of taking upon itself the burden and the responsibility of revolutionary initiatives and actions constantly being imposed by the pressing events. This explains the historical paradox by which the masses are the ones who push and "educate" the working class party and not the party that educates and guides the masses. . . . Actually, this Socialist Party, which proclaims itself the guide and master of the masses, is nothing but a humble notary who records the operations spontaneously performed by the masses. (Ibid., in ON, pp. 659–660)

If, in spite of all this, a catastrophe had been successfully averted for the workers' movement it was because "in the urban sections of the party, in the trade unions, in factories and villages, there exist vigorous groups of communists conscious of their historical mandate." Within the Socialist Party there was already a communist party, "which only lacks an explicit organization, centralization, and its own discipline so as to quickly develop itself, and to conquer and renew the party of the working class as a whole." On the basis of the theses approved by the Second Congress of the Third International, the communists had to work toward "forming the communist faction of the Italian socialist party in the shortest time possible." The party had to become "in name and deed the Italian Communist Party, a section of the Third Communist International" (ibid., in ON, pp. 660–661).

During August 1920, Gramsci founded a select group for "Communist Education." Challenging Togliatti and Terracini, he refused to join the pro-election faction [*elezionista*] of the socialist section of Turin. Despite warming relations during the days of the factory occupations, Gramsci remained isolated. With administrative elections approaching on October 31 and November 7, his candidacy was rejected by the socialist assembly and removed from the electoral list.

On November 28 and 29, a meeting was held at Imola during which the communist faction of the PSI was officially formed. Within this so-called "Imola faction," Bordiga's group emerged as the most influential. Having long been organized at the national level, the group was inclined toward separation from the party. Gramsci, present at the meeting, still called for an attempt at internal renewal.

December 24 marked the last issue of the weekly *Ordine Nuovo*; it became a daily paper on January 1, 1921, with Gramsci as director. It was replacing the Turin edition of *Avanti!*; *Ordine Nuovo*, Gramsci wrote, "will continue the aggressive tradition of the Socialist Party's newspaper, together with the brief but note-

worthy traditional activity of education and propaganda of the
weekly review" ("*Dal 1 gennaio 1921 L'Ordine Nuovo*" [From
January 1, 1921, *Ordine Nuovo*], in ON, p. 802). In reality,
"*Rassegna settimanale di cultura socialista*" [Weekly Review of
Socialist Culture] would remain an unrepeatable experience in
many ways. Its two-year lifespan coincided with one of the most
dramatic, but also most exciting, moments in the history of the
Italian workers' movement. In the pages of *Ordine Nuovo* were
reflected the crisis of the bourgeoisie and revolutionary fervor, as
well as a will for progress and reactionary surges. A communist
periodical is "the workers' blood and flesh," but intellectuals like
Giuseppe Prezzolini, Piero Gobetti, and Georges Sorel also
became involved in its affairs. Prezzolini would later say that the
weekly was full of:

> literary and revolutionary writings, better than those we used to
> find in the columns of socialist newspapers and periodicals. But
> managing to run a paper and throwing themselves into militant
> politics, in my view, dampened the creative qualities of the
> young group, whose original ingenuity and faith were coupled as
> rarely happens.

Prezzolini's criticism was certainly vitiated by a political pre-
conception. Nevertheless, there is no doubt that Gramsci's writings in the weekly *Ordine Nuovo* constitute, along with the
Notebooks, his most significant legacy in terms of theory.

On the eve of the PSI's 17th Congress on January 15, 1921,
Gramsci published "*Il Congresso di Livorno*" [The Livorno
Congress] in *Ordine Nuovo*:

> At Livorno it will be finally ascertained whether the Italian work-
> ing class has the ability to form an autonomous class party from
> its ranks; it will be finally ascertained whether the experiences of
> a four-year imperialist war and a two-year decline in the world's

production forces will convince the Italian workers of their historical mission. ("*Il Congresso di Livorno*," in SF, p. 39)

By then, the course undertaken by Bordiga and increasingly supported by Lenin was also openly accepted by Gramsci:

> The separation that will take place between communists and reformists in Livorno will have especially this meaning: the revolutionary working class is separating itself from those degenerate socialist tendencies that had rotted away within state parasitism, it is separating itself from those tendencies that were trying to exploit the North's advantageous position over the South to create proletarian aristocracies. . . . The revolutionary working class affirms its rejection of such spurious forms of socialism: workers' emancipation cannot be realized by snatching privileges, for a proletarian aristocracy, through parliamentary compromise and ministerial blackmail. Workers' emancipation can only occur with the alliance between industrial workers of the North and the poor peasants of the South for the overthrow of the bourgeois state and the establishment of the workers' and peasants' state. (Ibid., SF, pp. 40–41)

There were three tendencies that clashed at the Congress. The "unitarian maximalist" tendency was against separation from the reformists and backed the International. The other two were the reformist and the communist. The maximalist line, led by Serrati, advocated for the party's "maximum" program through revolutionary action for the immediate overthrow of the capitalist order and the full implementation of the socialist project. The maximalists received 98,028 votes, the reformists 14,695, and the communists 58,783. On January 21, the communists—among them Bordiga's "abstentionist" faction and the Piedmontese group of *Ordine Nuovo*—left the Congress's venue, the Goldoni Theater, and gathered at San Marco

Theater where they resolved to form the Italian Communist Party as a section of the Third International.

Amadeo Bordiga became the undisputed leader of the new party. Gramsci, who had not taken the floor in Livorno, was elected to the central committee, but excluded from the executive. His political status remained undefined. Only thirty years old at the time and little known in the party, Gramsci was above all renowned as an intellectual. It was only a few years later that he became well known as a prominent communist leader.

7. "In the first socialist country."

Commenting on the Livorno schism in "*Caporetto e Vittorio Veneto*" [Caporetto and Vittorio Veneto], Gramsci pointed out the dangers of the "particularly difficult period" during which the Communist Party was founded. "Indeed, it would have been preferable to have a strong workers' political organization today; it would have been preferable to be ready today to talk about action and no longer about preparation" ("*Caporetto e Vittorio Veneto*," in FS, pp. 50–51).

In *Ordine Nuovo*, he continued a stiff polemic with the PSI and began analyzing the nature and possible developments of fascism. "What is fascism if viewed through an international scale? It is an attempt to solve the problems of production and exchange with machine guns and rounds of gunfire" ("*Italia e Spagna*" [Italy and Spain], in SF, p. 101). In Italy, the revolutionary violence that "erupted simultaneously all over the national territory, spurred automatically the synchronized revolutionary efforts of the attacked masses" ("*Sangue freddo*" [Cold Blood], in SF, p. 88). With the absence of a political center capable of organizing and guiding the proletariat, blow-by-blow counterattacks against the blackshirts [*squadristi*] meant venturing into a spiral with unpredictable consequences. On the other hand:

socialists express horror at the prospect of civil war, as if socialism could be possible without civil war. They still believe in
their ability to fight the bourgeois class, which organizes and
sparks off violence everywhere, with parliamentary protest and
moves to censure fascist barbarities. (*"Socialisti e comunisti"*
[Socialists and Communists], in SF, p. 104)

Largely ahead of the socialists, but also of the members of his
very same party, Gramsci dangled the hypothesis of a coup d'état.
Entire provinces and regions were ruled by fascists, instead of the
official authorities. Even capital punishment had been reinstated,
administered de facto by "extralegal organizations."

> Parliament still exists, the government is still selected and con-
> trolled by parliament; no extraordinary laws have yet formally
> abolished statutory guarantees. But is it possible to imagine that
> such a situation can last for long? Today, there are two repressive
> and punitive apparatuses in Italy: fascism and the bourgeois
> state. A simple calculus of utility induces us to expect the domi-
> nant class to combine these two apparatuses at some point, even
> officially, and that will break up the resistance posed by the tra-
> ditional functioning of the state with a surprise attack against the
> central organs of government. (*"Colpo di Stato"* [Coup d'état], in
> SF, p. 258)

Gramsci wrote these lines in July 1921, when the "peace
treaty" negotiation was under way between socialist and fascist
members of parliament [*"I capi e le masse"* [Rulers and Masses],
in SF, p. 224).

> It is always good to remember that the outcome of the peace
> treaty has only resulted in curbing the outrage of the population
> at large, which was rising up against fascism, and to allow the lat-
> ter to improve its armed organizing efforts. Socialists were nei-

ther able to launch a call to arms nor to prepare, in the meantime, the start of a general proletarian offensive. Disoriented by
fascist violence they found themselves, after the peace treaty,
even more marginalized from any action. ("*Nella tregua*"
[During the Truce], in SF, p. 430)

"Passive resistance," in Gramsci's view, was "a silly phrase
that by now cannot but disgust the downtrodden spirit of those
who suffer under fascist terror" (ibid., SF, p. 431). Regardless,
the organization of armed resistance faced nearly insurmountable
odds. The workers' movement appeared ever more divided and
discouraged before increasing blackshirt intimidation. Even the
leadership of the International was acknowledging the radical
shift of terms in the "Italian question." Power relations were by
then unfavorable for the revolutionary proletariat. Predictions
about the ultimate success of the 1919–1920 struggles had not
come true. In an article dated March 1921, Zinoviev conceded
that "the tempo of the international proletarian revolution is
rather slowing down, due to a series of circumstances." In
December, the executive of the International, which supported
and favored the Livorno breakup, published its theses about a
"single workers' front" to oppose the reactionary offensive raging
all over Europe.

From December 18 to 20, Gramsci took part of an extended
meeting in Rome of the central committee of the Italian
Communist Party. The party's second congress was again held in
Rome from March 20–22. Meanwhile, a split was taking place
between Bordiga's leadership and the International. In Congress,
a large majority voted for the so-called "Roman theses," which
opposed the "single front" strategy. It was decided that Gramsci
would represent the party in Moscow, in the executive committee
of the Third International.

On May 26, [1922], Gramsci left Italy for the Soviet Union in
a state of physical exhaustion, worn out from a year's worth of

intense work. In June, he became a member of the Communist International's executive committee. Not long after this appointment, Gramsci was taken to the "*Serebryanyi bor*" [Silver Forest] sanatorium to regain his health. Here he met another patient, Eugenia Schucht, daughter of an exiled anti-tsarist, who had lived in Rome as a student. A friendly relationship developed between Gramsci and Eugenia during his long days at the sanatorium. Around the middle of June, he met her sister Julia, who was visiting. As a musician, she had also studied in Italy, taking violin classes at the Academy of Santa Cecilia in Rome. Later, he would write her that "I didn't dare enter the room, because I was intimidated by you" (D, pp. 11, 46; also in L, p. 361). Gramsci immediately fell deeply in love with this young woman. Julia Schucht would become his companion and bear him two children, Delio and Giuliano.

On September 8, 1922, Gramsci sent Trotsky, at his invitation, a letter on Italian futurism. The following year, it was published by Trotsky in "*Letteratura e rivoluzione*" [Literature and Revolution]. Interested in the futurist movement since his debut as a journalist ("*I futuristi*" [The Futurists], in CT, pp. 6–8), Gramsci drew a quick and vivid sketch about this movement that welded cultural and political analyses. The meaning of this short piece anticipates the content of his mordant definition in the *Notebooks*: "*The Futurists*. A group of little schoolboys who ran away from a Jesuit school, made some noise in the nearby woods, and were taken back under the stick of the forest ranger" (Q, p. 115).

On November 5, 1922, the Fourth Congress of the International began. The call for a "single front" against international reaction and for the defense of peace, wages, and jobs had already been rejected by the PCI [Communist Party of Italy]. The dispute between the Italian party and the Third International arose not so much over the content of the established strategy as much as the obligation that came with it to renew relations with the socialists and to once again consider them allies. The line taken up by Italian communists, in truth simply dictated by formal discipline, was to limit the application of the "single front" strategy to trade union action, excluding political alliances with other parties.

Bordiga's group insisted on safeguarding the identity of the PCI and its origin. Even after the October 28, 1922, march on Rome, the Bordighians failed to appreciate the risk of the fascist dictatorship they had incited. Gramsci, too, in spite of the greater depth of his analysis of fascism, was for sectarianism and the exclusion of socialists, as well as other non-communist movements, even if they were ready to meet fascist violence with armed struggle.

In contrast, Zinoviev's political report to the Congress recommended the merging of the Communist Party with the PSI. The new party would have been named the Unified Communist Party of Italy. A commission was appointed to carry out the merger, with Gramsci replacing Bordiga as a member. In fact, Bordiga was against the fusion, even after the Socialist Party's 19th Congress in Rome marked the breakup between the maximalist majority and the reformist wing. However, different viewpoints emerged within the party. Tasca favored adherence to the International's directives while Gramsci proposed a unification with only the "Third Internationalist" faction formed within the Socialist Party and not with the entire PSI. The proposal was accepted, but the unification project did not come into being.

Within a few months, a series of arrests decimated the leadership of the Italian left. Serrati was sent to jail. On February 3, 1923, it was Bordiga's turn. Tasca escaped to Switzerland. Gramsci remained in Russia to work in the executive of the International. He wrote to Julia:

> I will be stuck in Moscow for a while longer. The C.C. [Central Committee] of the P.C. [Communist Party] sent a cable warning of an arrest warrant issued against me in Italy, and of the impossibility of crossing the border illegally for now. (L, p. 113)

In June, the International's enlarged executive appointed the new executive committee of the PCI. This included Tasca, Togliatti, Mauro Scoccimarro, Giuseppe Vota, and Bruno Fortichiari (later replaced by Egidio Gennari). On September 21, the members of the committee were arrested in Milan; they were charged with plotting against the security of the state.

In November, it was decided that Gramsci should be transferred to Vienna, with the task of closely following the events related to the Italian party and maintaining the connections with the other European communist parties. His post in Moscow was filled by Terracini.

8. From Moscow to Vienna:
The Formation of the Executive of the PCI

Gramsci had been in Vienna since December 3, 1923. Though not officially the party head, he was undoubtedly its most prestigious leader.

His parting from Julia was a very painful event. Even in Moscow, the relationship between Gramsci and his companion had never been easy. Their meetings were filled with the uncertainty and anxiety of a sudden call to action. "They summon us at any time, at the least expected hours and I would be very displeased to miss a meeting without being able to justify my absence. I wish very much to come and say so many things to her. But will I be able to?" (L, p. 108).

Being far away and lonely, his longing for Julia was overbearing. "I live a very isolated life and it will be so for a long time. I miss you; I feel a great void around me. Today, more than yesterday and the day before yesterday, I know how much I love you and how I love you more with each passing day" (L, p. 144). Snow-covered Vienna was a melancholy sight: "the landscape is like a series of white piles that remind me of the Cagliari salt

mines and their convicts." The streets in Moscow were at least
plowed by "merry and shrilling" sleds, while in Vienna, there
were "only streetcars and their noise":

> My Dear, you have to come. I need you. I cannot live without
> you. You are a part of me and I feel I cannot live far from myself.
> I feel as if I am suspended in space, far from reality. I always
> remember with infinite regret the time we spent together, in so
> much intimacy, in such a great extension of ourselves. (D, pp.
> 11, 31; also in L, p. 193)

Julia would not be able to reach him. With pathetic pretexts,
she was keeping from him the signs of mental illness that would
wear her down for many years.

The PCI was in a very unstable organizational, political, and
theoretical situation. The communist militants, forced by then to
work in near total secrecy, were furthermore affected by the damaging effects of the party leadership's uncertainties and its ever
growing internal dissent. Bordiga had sent a highly critical appeal
of the International's line from prison. The absolute refusal to
collaborate with the PSI led him to question the very membership
of the Communist Party in the International. This time, Gramsci
did not go along with him. His Moscow experience had taught
him that the tie between his party and the International could not
be broken without serious consequences. The Soviet revolutionary example, and Lenin's mythical figure, represented possibly
the ultimate basis for the unity of the communist rank and file,
shattered as they were by fascist repression.

Gramsci's political reflections went so far as to fully rethink
the party's purpose, identity, and future:

> The political value of fusion. The forces of reaction have planned
> to push the proletariat back to the same conditions it endured
> during the initial phase of capitalism—dispersed, isolated, indi-

viduals, rather than a class that feels its unity and aspires to power. The Livorno breakup (the separation of the majority of Italian workers from the Communist International) has been undoubtedly the greatest success of reactionary forces. ("*Tre frammenti di Gramsci*" [Three Fragments of Gramsci], in PGD, p. 102)

On January 5, 1924, he wrote to Scoccimarro:

It is absolutely impossible to reach a compromise with Amadeo (Bordiga). He has too energetic a personality and he is so deeply convinced of being right that it would be an absurdity to think of netting him in a compromise. He will continue to fight and propose his same thesis again on every occasion.

He goes on to comment on the tiring discussions on the organization of the party:

instead of centralism, we turned into a pathological minority movement. Today we have to fight against extremists if we want the party to develop and cease to be nothing but an external faction of the Socialist Party. Indeed, the two extremisms, the right and the left, having constrained the party to a sole discussion on its relationship to the Socialist Party, have reduced it [the party] to a secondary role. I will probably remain alone. As a member of *Comitato Centrale* [Central Committee] (CC) and of the Comintern executive, I will write a report in which I will fight against the former and the latter, blaming both for this mistake. From the doctrine and strategy of Comintern, I will deduce a program of action for our future activity. ("*Lettera a Scoccimarro del 5 gennaio 1924*" [Letter of January 5, 1924, to Scoccimarro] in PGD, pp. 150–152; also in L, pp. 160–162)

In his letter to Togliatti and Terracini dated February 9, Gramsci fully explained his understanding of the party. Earlier he had cautiously evaluated the dangers of a possible fracture. And yet the time was ready "not only for a thorough discussion about our internal situation in front of the party's masses, but also about the formation of new groups that veer toward the party's leadership" ("*A Palmi, Urbani e C.*" [To Palmi, Urbani and C.], in PGD, p. 186; also in L., p. 223).

Gramsci denied that a crisis of trust existed between the International and the party at large. "Such a crisis exists only between the International and a section of the party leaders." Bordiga's convictions did not agree with those of the party's in general: he "wanted" them to become those of the party.

A new historical phase had begun "not only for our party, but also for our country." The communists' mistake had been to aim abstractly at resolving the organizational problem. It was believed that the revolution depended exclusively on the existence of "an apparatus of functionaries who closely adhered to the official line." This went so far as the belief that the simple existence of this apparatus could determine the revolution:

> Nothing was done to inspire among the masses, on every occasion, the potential for expressing themselves in line with the Communist Party. Every event, every local, national, or world anniversary should have been used to incite the masses through communist cells, by voting motions and spreading leaflets. This was not fortuitous. The Communist Party was even against the formation of factory cells. Mass participation in the party's activity and internal life, other than on great occasions and following formal orders from the center, was seen as a danger to unity and centralism. The party was not understood as a dialectical process where the spontaneous movement of the revolutionary masses converge with the center's determination for organizing and guiding. It was conceived only as something out of thin air that develops within and for itself and that the masses will grasp when the time is right and the crest of the revolutionary wave

will rise to the party's height, or when party center decides on an offensive and lowers itself to the level of the masses to incite and lead them to action. ("*A Palmi, Urbani e C.*," in FGD, p. 195; also in L, pp. 231–232)

Historically, a political party is never defined: "It will be defined when it becomes everyone and so disappears."

On February 12, 1924, the first issue of *L'Unità. Quotidiano degli operai e dei contadini* [Unity: The Workers' and Peasants' Daily] went to press in Milan. From August 12 it would become "*Organo del PCI*" [The Organ of the PCI], after the "*terzini*" [fullbacks] joined the party. The title had been suggested by Gramsci and was intended to underline the importance of the Southern Question and the solidarity between the Northern working class and Southern rural masses. From March 1, the third series of *Ordine Nuovo* was started: a biweekly review of workers' politics and culture, published in Rome. Gramsci was not very satisfied with the first issue. He would write to Julia about it: "It had already been written a month before, when it was published, and it was completed in a hurry, because it was thought it had to be published at once, immediately" (L, p. 298). In any case, the review was "well received." Many comrades became deeply attached to this glorious paper. In an editorial entitled "*Capo*" [Leader], Gramsci commemorated Lenin, who had passed away on January 21, as the "initiator of a new process of historical development." He asked, what does it mean to be a "leader" of the workers' party?

Are the leader and the party elements of the working class, a part of it, representing its most profound and vital interests and aspirations, or are they its outgrowth or a simple violent superimposition?

The Russian Communist Party, with Lenin as its leader, was so bound to the entire development of the Russian proletariat, and, thus, to the development of the entire Russian nation, that it is not even possible to imagine one without the other, the proletariat as dominant class without the Communist Party being the government party and, therefore, without the party's central committee being the inspiration of government policies, without Lenin being the head of state. . . . In the end, even the Russian bourgeois understood, though poorly, that Lenin could never become head of state and keep this appointment without proletarian rule, without the Communist Party being the government party. ("*Capo*," in CPC, p. 14)

In Italy, too, there was a "leader" that was idolized by official ideology: Benito Mussolini.

We are familiar with that face, and the rolling of those eyes in their sockets which, in the past, by their mechanical fierceness, used to make the bourgeoisie and now the proletariat ill to their stomach. We are familiar with his fist always clenched as a threat. We know all this mechanism, all this paraphernalia, and we understand how this can impress the young of the bourgeois schools and move them. It is very impressive, even at close range, and it astounds. But a "leader"? [He is] the perfect embodiment of the Italian petit bourgeois, a rabid and fiery blend of all the debris left on the national soil by centuries of foreign and Church domination: he could not become the leader of the proletariat. He became the leader of the bourgeoisie, who love fiery faces when they turn Bourbon again, and hope to see the working class as terrified as they were by the rolling of those eyes and the threatening clenched fist. (Ibid., in CPC, p. 15)

Lenin's enormous effort in rebuilding Russian society, fragmented by five years of war, occurred during a proletarian dictatorship, whose characteristics were expansionist and not repressive. "A constant movement is happening from the bottom up, a constant capillary change throughout society, a constant turnover of men." Arbitrariness and abuse of power were the foundation of Mussolini's government. His doctrine amounted to nothing but threats and to his horrific "physical mask" (ibid., in CPC, p. 16).

On April 6, 1924, Gramsci was elected member of the Chamber of Deputies for the Veneto electoral district. Ten days later, he would write to Julia:

> The elections went very well for us. News that the party received various positions is very good: we officially obtained 304,000 votes, in reality we certainly received more than double; the fascists thought to take them for themselves, by erasing the communist symbol and drawing a fascist one over it. When I think at what it cost workers and peasants to vote for me; when I think about the 3,000 workers in Turin who wrote down my name under the threat of the stick and the more than 3,000 in Veneto, mostly peasants, who did the same, and about how many of them were badly beaten, I think that this time it is worthwhile and meaningful to become a deputy. However, I think that to be a revolutionary deputy in a chamber with 400 drunk and constantly screaming monkeys will require a level of vocal power and physical resistance that is beyond me. But I will do the best I can. Some energetic and strong workers whom I know very well have been elected and I am counting on being able to carry out a not at all useless activity. (L, pp. 324–325)

Thanks to parliamentary immunity, after a two-year absence Gramsci could return to Italy. "That Sardinian hunchback, economics and philosophy professor, an undoubtedly powerful mind," in Mussolini's words, was set to become the most prominent antifascist figure.

9. "We must become a great party."

During the second half of May 1924, the first national conference of the PCI was held in Como. Togliatti made the political presentation. Gramsci delivered a critical note on Bordiga's
approach, which still prevailed among the majority of federal
secretaries.

The national elections had been marred by abuses of power
and vote rigging. Mussolini had scored an important success by
gaining the two-thirds of parliamentary seats required by law for
an absolute majority.

Nevertheless, the opposition enjoyed much popular support.
Antifascist resistance came out strengthened by the election
results. During the early sessions of the new legislature, Giacomo
Matteotti, secretary of the Unified Socialist Party, distinguished
himself for his fighting spirit and toughness. On June 10,
Matteotti was abducted and murdered. There soon appeared
strong evidence implicating the government and Mussolini for
the assassination, which sparked an acute political crisis.

On June 22, Gramsci wrote to Julia:

I live and continue to live unforgettable days. From newspapers
it is impossible to get the right impression of what is happening
in Italy. We were walking on an erupting volcano, when, without
anyone anticipating it, especially the fascists, ever sure of their
infinite power, the volcano suddenly erupted, unleashing an
immense river of ardent lava, sweeping away everything and
everyone fascist. Events were developing with unheard of light-
ning speed. From day to day, from hour to hour, the situation
was shifting. The regime was attacked from all sides. Fascism
was becoming isolated in the country. This became evident in its
leaders' panic and its followers' retreat . . . . Our movement has
made a great leap forward: the newspaper's circulation has tre-
bled, in many centers our comrades have placed themselves at

the head of the masses, and have tried to disarm the fascists. Our demands are welcomed with enthusiasm and repeated in the motions voted in the factories. In these days, I believe our party has become a real mass party. (L, pp. 356–357)

Gramsci was by now the head of the party. As secretary general at the central committee meeting of August 13–14, he presented a report on "*I compiti del partito comunista di fronte alla crisi della società capitalistica italiana*" [The Tasks of the Communist Party in the Face of the Crisis in Italian Capitalist Society].

His political argumentation was far-reaching and opened a new phase for the PCI. Even if the party's base was still under Bordiga's influence, the original abstract revolutionary rhetoric and sectarianism were rapidly fading away.

What should be our party's political direction and strategy in the present situation? The situation is "democratic" in that the working masses are disorganized, dispersed, and fragmented in the general indistinct population. Whatever immediate consequences the crisis will have, we can only anticipate an improvement in the workers' political position, not their triumphal struggle to power. The essential task of our party is to take over the reins of the majority of the working class; the transitional phase we are going through is not a direct struggle for power, but a preparatory stage, a transitional one in the struggle for power. It is in other words a phase of agitation, propaganda and organizing. . . . If groups or trends exist within our party that wish to force the situation out of fanaticism, we need to fight against them on behalf of the whole party, and the vital and permanent interests of the Italian proletarian revolution . . . therefore, we have to fight against any right-wing tendency that wants a compromise with the opposition, and that tries to hinder the revolutionary developments of our strategy and the preparatory activity for the following stage. ("*La crisi italiana*" [The Italian Crisis], in CPC, pp. 37–38)

Gramsci's conclusion was that it was necessary to become a great party so as:

> to attract the largest possible number of revolutionary workers
> and peasants to our organizations and to prepare them to fight,
> to turn them into mass organizers and leaders, and to elevate
> them politically. (Ibid.)

It needs to be remembered that "communist education" is a topic that was dear to Gramsci from the beginnings of his political life. In February 1925 he contributed to the formation of a correspondence-based party school, for which he was charged with lecture note duplication. Two of them would later appear in the spring of the same year. Thus, there was continuity of thought between the Gramsci of the councils and the secretary of the PCI. But, in little more than five years, the national and international political scene had changed drastically. Even in the most successful phase of expansion of the workers' movement, similar attempts to organize party schools had never gone beyond "the limited group, the small circle, the efforts of the isolated few." With the new stabilization of capitalism and the need to confront fascism by every means, the trust in the almost prodigious virtues of "culture" came to be set aside. If it was true that the young guard of *Ordine Nuovo* had believed in relying on abstract "Enlightenment" understandings, it was now a new reality that moved Gramsci's pedagogical project, which preserved very little of past idealistic tendencies. Culture and politics remained inseparable. However, culture lost its role as a universal guide for the creation of revolutionary action; it had become an "instrument" of political praxis:

> We are a fighting organization, and in our ranks we study to grow,
> to refine individuals' and the whole organization's ability to fight,
> to better understand the enemy's positions and ours, to better

adapt our daily activities to them. Learning and culture are nothing other than the theoretical conscience of our immediate and highest aims, and the way we can translate them into action ("*La scuola di partito*" [The Party School], in CPC, pp. 49–50).

Theoretical conscience and revolutionary doctrine were the party's decisive "weapons." But without a party no victory was possible. And it was to changing the organizational structure of the party, by now forced into semi-hiding, that Gramsci devoted himself until the third PCI Congress.

During the months preceding the January 1926 Lyon Congress, the Communist Party was becoming influential among the political factions intent on keeping up the struggle against fascist reaction. Its strength consisted primarily in denouncing the class character of fascism, linked to the high bourgeoisie, an accusation to which Gramsci had contributed in a determinant way. A common plan of action, which had also included the formation of a republican assembly based on worker and peasant committees, had been rejected by other parties of the left. Nevertheless, the unitary initiative, even if confused and vague, had been the only attempt at gathering the forces willing to fight for the establishment of a democratic republic. These objectives of political democracy had not yet been clearly formulated by the PCI. The proposal for worker and peasant committees as a unified front from below, rather than just an alliance among the parties' leaders, nevertheless gained approval. Mass unified action had been unfolding during 1925. The *Unità* newspaper was getting support from non-communist workers, too, while party membership was increasing. And the communist presence was felt in factories and public rallies.

It was in this political climate, August to September 1925, that Gramsci, together with Togliatti, prepared to present their thesis in Lyon. It opened with an in-depth historical examination of "Italian social structure," of the "politics of the Italian bourgeoisie" and of fascism as "the instrument of an industrial and rural oligarchy for centralizing the control of all national wealth in the hands of capital" (*"La situazione italiana e il compito del PCI"* [The Italian Situation and the Task of the PCI], in CPC, p. 496). The right stood by its uncompromising position, which primarily affected the PSI [Italian Socialist Party]. Nevertheless, the central topic evaluated by the Congress was that concerning the *alliances* of the party. "The driving forces of the Italian revolution . . . are the following, in order of importance: 1) the working class and the agricultural proletariat; 2) the peasants of Southern Italy and the islands and of other parts of Italy" (ibid., in CPC, p. 498).

Speaking at the political committee meeting, held on January 20th on the eve of the Congress, Gramsci states:

> In no country is the proletariat capable of gaining power and keeping it solely by means of its own forces. It must therefore find allies. That is, it must carry out a type of policy that enables it to lead other classes with anti-capitalistic interests and guide them in the fight against bourgeois society. The problem is of particular importance in Italy, where the proletariat is a minority of the working population, and, geographically, is positioned in such a way that only after finding a solution to the problem of its relationship with the peasant class can it expect to carry out a successful fight for power. In the future, our party should devote itself to the formulation and solution of this problem. (*"Il congresso di Lione. Intervento alla commissione politica"* [The Lyon Congress: Speech to the Political Committee], in CPC, p. 483)

The entire listing of the new executive led by Gramsci was approved in Lyon. It received 90.8 percent of the votes, against 9.2 for Bordiga's left.

It has sometimes been noted that the Third Congress of the PCI could be considered the actual constitutive congress of the party. In fact, it is after Lyon that it succeeded in undertaking a political direction, at once harsh with respect to struggles and sacrifices, but rich in experiences and future developments.

10. The Southern Question

Among the members elected in the Third Congress to the Central Committee, the political office, and the secretariat were Gramsci (as general secretary), Togliatti, Tasca, Terracini, Bordiga, Scoccimarro, Camilla Ravera, Ruggero Grieco and Alfonso Leonetti. Serrati was also in the central committee. After the latter's death, Gramsci published an article in the May 14 issue of *Unità* where he recalled, with reserve and great equanimity, the story of the polemics within the Socialist Party, until Serrati joined the PCI. "Comrade Serrati died in the top ranks of the Communist Party of Italy and in the top ranks of the Communist International" ("*Giacinto Menotti Serrati,*" in CPC, p. 113).

The fate of the executive formed in Lyon was to be tragic. After only a year, half of the members of the central committee fell into the hands of the fascist police.

Antonio Gramsci was arrested in Rome on November 8, 1926. The "exceptional measures" adopted by the regime had nullified parliamentary privilege. For the communist thinker it was the beginning of a decade of terrible hardship and unheard-of physical and moral suffering.

Gramsci's arrest took place during a period of feverish activity. On October 14, on behalf of the PCI, he had sent Togliatti—who was in Moscow at the time—a letter titled "*Al Comitato centrale del Partito comunista sovietico*" [To the Soviet Communist Party's Central Committee]. It was a document of great importance that arrived during an extremely critical phase in the Bolshevik party's internal strife between the majority and its opposition. In the name of the Italian communists, Gramsci wrote:

Today, we no longer have the security we once had in the past. We feel irresistibly anguished. It seems to us that the present attitude of the opposition block and the sharpness of the Soviet Communist Party's debates call for the intervention of fraternal parties. ("*Al Comitato centrale del Partito comunista sovietico,*" in CPC, p. 125)

Gramsci pointed to the serious repercussions of a possible split within the Soviet party's executive. Lenin's warnings about studying enemy class positions already enabled one to foresee how the international bourgeoisie would look at the conflict with the conviction that "it must bring proletarian dictatorship to its disintegration and slow agony," and to "the revolution's catastrophe." The intensity of the crisis and the threat of a split interrupted the process of developing parties joining the International, crystallized "right and left deviations," and delayed "once again the successful development of the organic unity of the workers' world party."

Comrades, during these nine years of world history, you have been the organizing and driving element of all the countries' revolutionary forces: the function you carried out is unprecedented in scope and depth in all the history of mankind. However, today you are destroying your work; you are degrading yourself, running the risk of nullifying the leadership that the Soviet Union's Communist Party conquered under Lenin's drive; it seems to us that the violent passion you have for Russian problems makes you lose sight of the international aspects of those very same Russian problems. It makes you forget that your duties as Russian militants can and must be fulfilled only within the framework of the international proletariat." (Ibid., in CPC, p. 128)

On October 18, Togliatti, who had shown the letter only to Bukharin, expressed his disagreement with the positions voiced by Gramsci. He conceded that the latter had correctly indicated the opposition as "the most responsible" for the situation within the Soviet party, that is, Zinoviev, Kamenev, and Trotsky. Nevertheless, Togliatti considered Gramsci's judgment to be unbalanced. In fact, it appeared that "the Italian Communist Party's political office considers everyone responsible, and to be called to order" ("*Togliatti e Gramsci, 18 ottobre 1926*" [Togliatti and Gramsci, October 18, 1926], in CPC, p. 132). This seemed to extend even to the majority led by Bukharin and Stalin. "Can we state that some of the blame falls on the Central Committee? I don't think so," Togliatti wrote. Gramsci's viewpoint was considered "too pessimistic." However, this was not the only case in which such a pessimistic view would be proven correct by the facts.

In his answer to Togliatti dated October 26, Gramsci assured him that the letter to the Central Committee of the Bolshevik party "was nothing other than a closing speech against the opposition." There should be no concern if the fight for unity can benefit "*even* the opposition":

> The Leninist line consists of fighting for party unity, not only its outer unity, but also a more internal one where there is no chance for the development of two completely divergent political lines within the party regarding all questions. Party unity is essential not only in all our countries, as far as the International's political ideology is concerned, but in Russia as well, as far as proletarian *hegemony*, that is, the state's social content, is concerned. ("*Gramsci e Togliatti, 26 ottobre 1926*," in CPC, p. 135)

The term "hegemony" can be taken as signaling the substantial transformation that began to take shape in Gramsci's work at this time. The concept of hegemony is fundamental in the study and interpretation of Gramsci's work. The term recurs frequently in his prison writings, but until then it had rarely appeared in his newspaper articles. In *Ordine Nuovo* of March 1, 1921—an issue devoted entirely to Lenin—one reads: "In the international history of class struggle, it is Bolshevism that first developed the idea of proletarian hegemony." Conceived historically and concretely, the idea of proletarian hegemony "brought with it the need to find an ally for the working class; Bolshevism found this ally in the mass of poor peasants." The concept of Bolshevism, first proposed by Lenin in his "two social democratic strategies in the democratic revolution," found support in the development of the Italian workers' movement after the factory occupation of 1920:

> Poor peasants all over Italy, especially those in Southern Italy and the islands, needed land, but they were too ignorant, too isolated in their villages and hamlets to resist the concentrated attacks of fascist troops, which were being organized in the city. Only with the help of workers, only a close alliance between worker and peasant could the situation be remedied. . . . Peasants cannot conquer the land without workers' help. Workers cannot overthrow capitalism without peasants' help. However, the worker is politically stronger, more capable than a peasant; he lives in the city and is massively concentrated in factories. He is not only capable of overthrowing capitalism, but also of preventing its return by socializing industry. This is why revolution is virtually under the hegemony of the proletariat, who leads its peasant ally, that is, the peasant class. ("*Vladimiro Ilic Ulianof*," in ON, third series, year 1, no. 1, March 1924)

The term "hegemony" was used not only by Lenin but also by Bukharin, Zinoviev, and Stalin, and it appeared in various documents of the International. Without entering the debate on the more or less Leninist origin of Gramsci's concept of hegemony, it is of interest to underline that Gramsci's research assumed a different character through a systematic use of this notion. The let-

ter to the Soviet party's central committee occurred in the immediacy of a political polemic, which formed the privileged ground
and main stimulus of Gramsci's newspaper writings. During the
same month, Gramsci wrote the essay *"Alcuni temi della quistione
meridionale"* [Some Themes on the Southern Question]. This
text marks Gramsci's transition to the type of work and research
he later fully implemented in *The Prison Notebooks*. In a letter
dated December 15, 1930, Gramsci said:

> It may be because my entire intellectual background has been of
> a polemical type; even "disinterested" thinking is difficult for
> me. That is, I study for the sake of studying. Only sometimes,
> though rarely, do I lose myself in a determined order of reflec-
> tions and find, so to speak, in the things themselves an interest
> in examining them. Generally, I have to place myself in a dialog-
> ical and dialectical perspective. Otherwise I am not intellectually
> stimulated. As I once told you, I do not like to throw stones in
> the darkness. I want to listen to an interlocutor or a real adver-
> sary. (LC, p. 374)

In fact, the incomplete text on the Southern Question—first
published in Paris in *Lo stato operaio* [The Workers' State] in
1930—opens with a polemic. Gramsci's "stones" were thrown
against the editorial board of *Quarto Stato* [Fourth Estate] for
criticizing the Communist Party's position on the problems of
Southern Italy by reducing it to the "magical formula" of the mere
mechanical distribution of large agricultural land among the rural
proletarians. In reality, since the time of *Ordine Nuovo*, the crux of
the matter for the Communists was establishing a political
alliance between northern workers and southern peasants.
According to Gramsci, the land-to-peasants formula, therefore,
had to be placed in the context of "a general revolutionary action
by the two allied classes, under the leadership of the industrial
proletariat," so that:

... revolutionary workers in Turin and Milan would become the protagonists of the Southern Question.

The Communists in Turin had pragmatically asked themselves the question of "proletarian hegemony," that is, of the social foundation of proletarian dictatorship and the workers' state. The proletariat can become the ruling and dominant class to the extent that it succeeds in forming a system of class alliances that makes it possible to mobilize the majority of the working population against capitalism and the bourgeois state. This means, in Italy, under actual class relations in Italy, the ability to obtain the support of large peasant masses. ("*Alcuni temi della questione meridionale*" [Some Themes on the Southern Question], in CPC, pp. 139–140)

However, for Gramsci, the peasant question was "historically determined" in Italy. It was not a "general" agrarian question. In the specific development of national history, it took on two particular forms: the Southern Question and the Vatican Question (regarding the influential presence of the Church in Italian history). The Italian proletariat, therefore, must make them its own, inserting them in its "transitional revolutionary program."

Gramsci tested some theoretical principles in his essay on the Southern Question that would be further refined and used in the *Prison Notebooks*. The southern "agrarian block" consisted of three social strata: the large mass of peasants, the low- and middle-class intellectuals, and the landowners and great intellectuals. The disaggregation of the peasants prevented any "centralized" expression of popular aspirations and needs. The totality of social ferment and protest was dominated by the great landowners in the political field and by the intellectuals in the ideological one.

Naturally, it is in the ideological field that centralization occurs with greater efficacy and precision. Giustino Fortunato and

Benedetto Croce, therefore, represent turnkeys of the southern system and, to a certain extent, they are the greatest figures of Italian reaction. (Ibid., CPC, p. 150)

The function of intellectuals within the bourgeois hegemonic system became very prominent. Since the very beginning, Gramsci's theory of hegemony exhibited a wide margin of autonomy with respect to the concept of the dictatorship of the proletariat. These two ideas were not irreconcilable, but hegemony could be applied to any social class—including the bourgeoisie.

The southern intellectual "is democratic with peasants, but reactionary with great landowners and the government" (ibid., CPC, p. 151). He formed a connection between peasants and landowners. This type of organization resulted in "a hideous agrarian bloc" that was not limited to local social relationships. It functioned "as intermediary and supervisor of northern capitalism and large banks" (ibid., CPC, p. 153).

Although Southern Italy lacked an organization of popular culture, there still existed "large accumulations of culture and intelligence in single individuals or in restricted groups of great intellectuals" (ibid., CPC, p. 155). Better still, the influence of southern intellectuals was constant on a national scale as well. Personalities like Fortunato and above all Croce, connected to the European cultural mainstream, had the necessary talent to tutor the well-educated youth of the South. Croce's philosophy had actualized a "historical" reform, changing traditional horizons and methods of thought and constructing a new worldview:

In this sense, Benedetto Croce fulfilled a very important "national" function. He separated southern radical intellectuals from the peasant masses by making them participants of national and European culture through which they became an integral part of the national bourgeoisie and, therefore, of the agrarian bloc. (Ibid., CPC, p. 156)

The *Ordine Nuovo* group came under Croce's influence as well. At the same time, however, it represented "a total break from that tradition and the beginning of a new development." The mediation exercised by the Turin communists between proletarians and certain intellectual strata of the left succeeded in modifying remarkably the latter's mentality. Gramsci's exemplary figure was Piero Gobetti, who "was not a communist, and, very likely, would have never become one, but understood the social and historical position of the proletariat and was no longer able to think outside of this element" (ibid., CPC, p. 156). Gobetti's intellectual loyalty became evident when contributing to the second series of *Ordine Nuovo*, as a theater and literary critic. An extraordinary cultural organizer, Gobetti represented a new historical climate and movement against which, on principle, one ought to struggle. "Not understanding this means being unable to understand the question related to intellectuals and their active participation in the class struggle" (ibid., CPC, p. 157). Naturally, intellectuals develop at a much slower pace than any other social group. As representatives of people's cultural tradition, they cannot suddenly break with the past and automatically adhere to a new ideology. However, it is of the greatest importance that there be "a fracture of organic characteristics" among intellectuals, that there be "a leftist tendency, in the modern sense of the term, oriented toward the revolutionary proletariat" (Ibid., CPC, p. 158).

The intellectual bloc's armor is "flexible but highly resistant to the agrarian bloc." It is only through its disaggregation that it is possible to develop a new "historical bloc."

The *Letters from Prison*

1. A Book that Belongs to All

Antonio Gramsci's *Letters from Prison* "belongs even to those of the opposition political party." These words were written by Benedetto Croce upon the publication of the first edition of Gramsci's correspondence, to which he added:

> It belongs to him for a twofold reason: for the respect and affection felt by all those who have a high regard for man's dignity and accept danger, persecution, suffering, and death for an ideal . . . and because, as a man of thought, he was one of us, one of those Italians who tried to form a philosophical and historical perspective adequate to the problems of the present. ("*Quaderni della 'Critica'*" [the Notebooks of "Criticism"], no. 8, July 1947)

In reality, this opinion is placed in a rather debatable context. The Neapolitan philosopher, in fact, was trying to wrest Gramsci from the Marxist tradition and the Communist Party's political-cultural orientation of the time. But it is difficult to believe that there was not a good dose of frankness in Croce's opinions—sincerity, but also surprise regarding Gramsci's private texts. "In reading his many judgments on men and books, I happened to agree with most of them, or, perhaps, all of them."

The *Letters from Prison* appeared in 1947, two years after the end of the antifascist war and ten years after the death of the Sardinian revolutionary. Much was expected from the publication of Gramsci's unedited writings. In any case, Croce's surprise was shared by most readers, who were amazed by the very high level of ethical, civil, and literary content. It was far from being a monotonous, more or less rhetorical and moving prison memoir. They were vivid pages, filled with humanity and thoughtfulness that allow us to gain access to Gramsci's emotional sphere and most intimate reflections. At the same time, they help us follow important phases in the origin and development of *The Notebooks*. The letters, among others by Gramsci the writer, do not constitute expression itself, but rather form an integral part of the elements necessary to reconstruct its "thought in development."

The first edition of his prison letters consisted of 218 documents. Others were later published in various newspapers and reviews. In 1964, the anthology *2000 pagine di Gramsci* [2000 Pages of Gramsci], published by il Saggiatore, included 77 new letters. The following year, the most comprehensive edition was published by Einaudi Editore, which consisted of 428 letters, 119 of which were unedited. Finally, six more letters appeared in 1986, in the book *Nuove lettere di Antonio Gramsci* [New Letters by Antonio Gramsci] published by Editori Riuniti.

Most of Gramsci's letters, written soon after his arrest, were addressed to his family: to his wife Julia and his sons, his mother, his sisters, his brother Carlo and his sister-in-law Tatiana Schucht. A small number of them were addressed to his friends. On the other hand, except for his short period of confinement in Ustica, Gramsci's correspondence was subject to prison restrictions. From Milan, he could write two letters a week; from Turi, at first, one every fifteen days and then one every week, but only to his relatives.

Particularly notable was his correspondence with his sister-in-law Tatiana. Gramsci had the opportunity to meet her in 1925, as he recalled in a letter to Julia in February of the same year: "I met your sister Tatiana. Yesterday, we spent time together from 4 o'clock in the afternoon to almost midnight. . . . I believe we are already good friends" (L, p. 412). With a degree in the natural sciences, Tatiana was teaching at an international institute in Rome. During Gramsci's imprisonment, she was the closest person to him. She visited him in Milan and at Turi, and assisted him until the end at the clinics where he was admitted after his release from prison.

We must not forget another figure, Piero Sraffa, who, with extreme discretion and concern, made every effort to give moral and material support to his friend, who was stricken by serious adversities. Sraffa, an eminent scholar, professor of political economy at Cambridge since 1927, had sided with the Turin socialist group and contributed to the weekly *Ordine Nuovo*. Although Sraffa's presence was not always mentioned in Gramsci's prison letters, he was often Gramsci's real interlocutor. As already mentioned above, rules at Turi prison allowed inmates to exchange letters only with family members. Therefore, Gramsci's correspondence was copied by Tatiana and sent to Sraffa, who, in turn, suggested ideas and topics for the replies. The complex dialogue between Gramsci and Sraffa is best exemplified by Tatiana's letter of August 28, 1931. In this letter, she was suggesting that Gramsci devote himself to his own project on the history of intellectuals and not be bothered by "excessive scientific scruples" and the inconvenience of not having a "large library" at his disposal (AP, pp. 235–237). This letter faithfully restated the observations expressed in the one sent by Sraffa to Tatiana on August 23 (LTG, pp. 21–24). Writing again to his sister-in-law a few days later, Gramsci pointed out: "I understand that you spoke with

Piero, because he is the only one who can tell you such things"
(LC, p. 457).

It can be said that both Sraffa and Tatiana collaborated in
stimulating Gramsci intellectually during his periods of crisis and
intellectual inertia. Many letters of this economist, still unpublished, highlight an intense, although indirect, exchange of ideas
with Gramsci. They discussed science and philosophy,
Machiavelli's concepts of economy, David Ricardo's theories relative to modern thought, showing different and at times sharply
contrasting opinions. Aside from this, Sraffa remained close to
"Nino" [the diminutive for Antonio] throughout his ordeals. He
would later make every effort to get the case reviewed and struggle until the very end to bring Gramsci's merciless prison conditions to international attention.

Sraffa's contribution to alleviating some of the tragic aspects
of Gramsci's vicissitudes in prison was very noble. Even the literary work of the Communist leader owes much to the concerned
interest of his friend. In fact, it is because of Sraffa's generosity
that Gramsci was able to have a reference library to support his
solitary reflections. It is also thanks to Sraffa that the *Notebooks*
were safeguarded immediately after the author's death.

Gramsci was posting letters from solitary confinement to two
vastly different worlds: Sardinia, where his family lived, and the
Soviet Union, where Julia was raising Delio and Giuliano. The
fusion of these contexts, so different from one another, is highly
suggestive. The memories of his childhood and the traditions of
his native land are intertwined very attentively with the social
order and the development of the first socialist country. With
extraordinary sensitivity, quotidian experience is united with the
tenderness of affection, lived through both a motionless past and
a possible future that no longer appear as opposites.

2. "Studying even under the most difficult conditions."

In the opening letter from the *Letters from Prison*, addressed to Clara Passarge, whose family hosted Gramsci in Rome, the following request appears:

I would like to have these books:

1. The German grammar that was on the shelf next to the entrance;
2. *Breviario di linguistica* [Survey of Linguistics] by Bertoni and Bartoli that was in the wardrobe in front of the bed;
3. Shall be very grateful if you send me a cheap edition of the *Divina commedia* [The Divine Comedy] because I have lent my own. (LC, p. 3)

At the time of his arrest, Gramsci had a note for the editorial staff of *l'Unità* in his pocket, in which he maintained that it was necessary to get used "to think and study even under the most difficult conditions." To keep the risk of "intellectual degradation" at bay was his most urgent concern.

On December 19, 1926, he wrote to Tatiana from Ustica:

On 19 November, I was notified of the order that condemned me to five years of solitary confinement in the colonies, with no explanation. The following days, the news spread that I would have left for Somalia. Only on the evening of the 24 did I get to know indirectly that I would have been exiled to an Italian island. (LC, p. 16)

The day after having learned that he would have been assigned to internal exile, he sent reassuring words to his family from Regina Coeli [Prison]. "I am and I will be strong; I love you very much and I want to see our little children again," he wrote to Julia. To his mother he added:

I am very calm and serene. Morally, I was prepared for everything. I will try to overcome, even physically, the difficulties that
I may encounter and to remain stable. You know my character,
so you know that fundamentally there is always a bit of humor
deep down in it; it will help me stay alive. (LC, pp. 5, 6)

The short period spent on the island was relatively positive
for Gramsci. "Ustica will be for me a pleasant enough stay from
the point of view of animal life," he confided to Sraffa, "because
the climate is excellent and I can take healthy walks."

He was housed in a private home together with five other
political exiles, including Bordiga. The friendly atmosphere and
the cordial relationship with his comrades were recalled with
comfort in some of his letters: the processing of small everyday
matters, the table and the kitchen, and the evening card games.
He also organized a school for general culture, of which he
headed the historical-literary section, while Bordiga was
entrusted with the scientific one.

On January 14, 1927, Gramsci was issued a warrant from the
military tribunal of Milan. He left Ustica "the morning of the 20,
suddenly." The journey lasted 19 days; it seemed to him like a
"very long film."

I want to give to you the whole picture of this train journey, as in
a very slow motion train. Imagine that an immense worm twists
its way from Palermo to Milan, constantly breaking up and
recomposing itself, leaving in every prison part of its rings, forming new ones again, flinging its formations to the right and left
and reincorporating the extractions. This worm has some lairs
in every prison, called transits, where we stop from 2 to 8 days.
These transits pile up, forming a lump, the filth and misery of
generations. We arrive tired, dirty, with wrists pained by long
hours of being chained, with a long beard, unkempt hair, sunken
and glistening eyes from the excitation of the will and from

insomnia. We jump on straw pallets who knows how old, with our clothes on, so as not to have contact with the filth, enveloping our faces and hands in our own towels, covered with blankets, good enough to avoid freezing. We leave again for a new transit, even dirtier and more tired, our wrists even more bruised because of the cold irons, the heavy chains, and the fatigue from carrying our luggage so burdened. (LC, p. 42)

On February 7, Gramsci was locked up in solitary confinement in the San Vittore judicial prisons. He remained in Milan until May the following year. The preliminary investigation proceeded very slowly: it was not an easy task to find objective evidence for the charges against generic subversive activities. A report of the Carabinieri of Rome even resorted to certifying a denunciation of November 1922 against Gramsci as being "found in possession of weapons and explosives." It should be recalled that on that date the Communist leader was in Moscow for a few months and had been admitted to the sanatorium.

In March, he informed Tatiana of his own study and working plan (letter of March 19, 1927):

My life unfolds always equally monotonous. Even studying is much more difficult than it would seem. I received some books, and in reality I read very much (more than a book a day, besides newspapers), but it is not to this that I am referring. It is something else. I am dogged by this idea (this phenomenon is typical for those in prison, I think): that we should do something '*für ewig*' [for eternity]. (LC, p. 55)

It would take two more years before Gramsci would begin drafting the *Notebooks*. The ideas, insights, and projects were already displayed in his letters. Reading an article in a magazine or book, casual conversations with other prisoners became occasions for rich and stimulating reflections. It was the case, for example, of a "small 'prison' debate" in February 1928 that led Gramsci to anticipate a phenomenon which to this day still affects, to a considerable extent, the customs and the culture of large sections of society—especially the youth.

To a fellow prisoner, concerned about a possible influence of Asian religions on European culture, Gramsci replied that the real "danger" is not from the East; attention must rather be given to the influence of African-American music:

> This music has really conquered a whole layer of the well-edu-
> cated European population; indeed, it has created a true zeal.
> Now, it is impossible to imagine that the constant repetition of
> physical gestures by Blacks dancing around their fetishes and
> that having the syncopated rhythm of jazz bands always in one's
> ears have no ideological results: a) this is an enormously wide-
> spread phenomenon that affects millions and millions of indi-
> viduals, especially the young; b) these are very strong and vio-
> lent impressions, that is to say that they leave deep and lasting
> traces; c) they are musical phenomena, that is, manifestations
> expressed in the most universal language existing today, a lan-
> guage that most quickly communicates a totality of images and
> impressions. (LC, p. 162)

3. "*Cavar sangue anche da una rapa.*"
[Wringing blood even from a stone.]

At the end of April, Gramsci was informed that the trial would be prosecuted in Rome on May 28, 1928, before the Special Court for the Defense of the State. He wrote to Tatiana: "This recent news somewhat excites me, but in a pleasant way. I feel more vibrant with life. I take it that there will be some struggle involved. Even if for but a few days, I will be in an environment different from that of prison" (LC, p. 185).

On May 10, on the eve of his departure, Gramsci wrote his mother asking her to try hard to understand, "as well with feeling," his own position as a political prisoner: "I will never be ashamed of this." After all:

> I myself, in a certain way, wanted my detention and conviction because I never wanted to change my views for which I would be willing to give my life and not only to stay in prison. (LC, p. 190)

Later, he would reiterate:

> I do not want to be pitied; I was a fighter who did not have any luck with his immediate fight, and fighters cannot and must not be pitied when they fought not because they were forced, but because they wanted to do so willingly. (LC, p. 448)

This conviction will accompany Gramsci throughout his ordeal, even in moments of great physical and moral suffering. Proof of this is the coherent firmness with which he refused to bow to sign a request for a pardon or ask for any act of clemency. Nevertheless, he asserted the "eminently practical" sense of his own attitude concerning prison conditions. No useless external gesture, but, on the contrary, a detailed search for all legal ways that could make his confinement less painful. He would never aspire to become a "new Gandhi who wants to demonstrate before the celestial and the underworld the torments of the Indian people" (LC, p. 331).

The so-called "big case" brought against the leadership of the Italian Communist Party ended on June 4. Among the defendants were Terracini, Scoccimarro, Giovanni Roveda, and Ezio Riboldi. During the questioning, Gramsci declared: "I am a communist and my political activity is well known as having been carried out publicly as parliamentarian and as a writer of *l'Unità*. . . . If being a Communist involves responsibility, I accept it." And lastly, addressing the judges: "You will bring Italy

to ruin, and it will be for us Communists to save her." On June 2,
the prosecutor, in his fierce indictment, pronounced the following sadly famous phrase: "For twenty years we must prevent this
brain from functioning." And so Gramsci was condemned to
twenty years, four months, and five days of prison, charged guilty
of crimes of insurrection, conspiracy, incitement to class hatred,
and civil war.

Affected by chronic uricemia, he was transferred to the Turi
special prison. He arrived there on July 19, after a new harrowing
journey through "ordinary transit":

> I was incredibly sick. I spent two hellish days and nights in
> Benevento. I was twisting like a worm; I couldn't stay seated, not
> even standing or lie down. The doctor told me that it was Saint
> Anthony's fire and there was nothing that could be done. (LC,
> pp. 199–200)

Gramsci was given the serial number 7047 and housed in a
dormitory together with five other political prisoners. He was suffering from depression and insomnia. In August, he obtained a
transfer to an individual prison cell; in January 1929, he received
the authorization to write. "Now that I can take notes, I want to
read according to a plan and study certain subjects and no longer
'devour' books" (LC, p. 236). On February 8th, he began to take
down notes for the first of the *Prison Notebooks*.

In the letters that follow, in the long list of books he requested,
and in his comments on cultural issues and problems, one can see
a progressive unfolding of Gramsci's research project. He was
proud to be able "to wring blood even from a stone," frequenting
the "disconnected" prison libraries. "In Milan," he recounted, "I
have read a certain number of all genres of books, especially popular novels." When one succeeds in organizing and annotating
readings according to a definite project, even shoddy works can
be useful, not only as diversionary reading.

I found that even Sue, Montépin, and Ponson du Terrail, etc., are enough if read with this question in mind: "Why is this literature always the most read and printed? What needs and aspirations does it serve? What feelings and viewpoints do such bad books represent that they are liked so much?" (LC, p. 254)

These are clearly some of the questions that Gramsci would try to answer in the *Notebooks* dedicated to literary criticism.

4. "Pessimism of intellect, and optimism of the will."

In "*Discorso agli anarchici*" [Speech to the Anarchists], published in April 1920 in *Ordine Nuovo*, Gramsci said that the socialist understanding of revolutionary process is characterized by "two fundamental features" and summarized in Romain Rolland's motto "pessimism of intellect and optimism of the will" ("*Discorso agli anarchici*," ON, p. 490). In December 1929 he wrote to his brother Carlo: "My state of mind summarizes these two feelings and overcomes them: I am a pessimist as to intellect, but an optimist as to will" (LC, p. 298).

During the same period, there is an appeal in Notebook 1 to "make people sober and patient, who do not become dejected before the worst horrors and do not grow excited for every foolish thing. Pessimism of intellect and optimism of the will" (Q, p. 75).

His attitude toward pessimism and optimism is later summarized in a comment in Notebook 9:

It should be noted that optimism, very often, is nothing but a way to defend one's own laziness, irresponsibility, and unwillingness to do anything. It is also a form of fatalism and mechanicism. One counts on factors beyond his own will and industriousness; they are exalted. It seems they are burned at some sacred altar of enthusiasm. And enthusiasm is nothing but superficial adoration of fetishes, a necessary reaction that must have the intellect as a starting point. The only justifiable enthusiasm is that which accompanies intelligent intention, intelligent industriousness, a wealth of inventiveness in concrete initiatives that bring change to existing reality. (Q, pp. 1191–1192)

Rolland's principle, which Gramsci led us to believe inspired his own way of living and thinking, can be taken as a model of the changes that the prison system produced on his character with the passing of years:

> Until some time ago, I was, so to speak, a pessimist concerning intellect, and an optimist as to will. That is, although I clearly saw all the unfavorable conditions and all strongly unfavorable ones relative to any improvement in my situation . . . I thought regardless that by rational effort, carried out with patience and care, without neglecting anything in organizing the few favorable elements and trying to neutralize the innumerable unfavorable ones, it was possible to achieve some substantial result, to be able at least to survive physically, to stop the terrible consumption of vital energies that is progressively exhausting me. Today, I do not think so. (LC, p. 717)

These lines are from May 1933. In the summer of two years earlier, Gramsci had been affected by a first serious health crisis. "It began this way: 3rd August, at one o'clock in the morning . . . all of a sudden, I began bleeding" (LC, p. 444). Then another crisis occurred on March 7, 1933. "Just last Tuesday, early in the morning, when I got up from bed, I fell down and I was not able to stand up by myself" (LC, p. 696). Gramsci's psycho-physical condition was by now irrevocably damaged:

> During the first days, I suffered from some curious pathological signs, which I partly remember and were partly described

to me by those who were present. For example, I spoke at
length in a language that nobody understood, and it certainly
was Sardinian dialect, because until a few days ago I realized
that I was unconsciously mixing Sardinian phrases and words
in my Italian. The room's windows and walls appeared
crowded with figures to me, especially faces; without being
frightful, they were, rather, in the most varied expressions,
smiling, and so on. Instead it seemed that, from time to time,
some compact but fluid masses that formed in the air accumu-
lated and then fell on me, forcing me, with a nervous thump,
back into bed. (LC, p. 698)

His general debilitation had reached its apex. On July 2, he
wrote to Tatiana with distressing words: "I am deprived of
strength. My last effort and breath of life was in January."

Time is a monstrous force; in prison, it is "a simple pseudonym for life itself" (LC, pp. 724–725).

Gramsci, however, was well aware of the effects of the "thin
file" that would wear him down, well before his bodily collapse
would force him to surrender. In a letter of October 20, 1928, he
wrote to Tatiana:

I would like to explain to Julia and you my general state of
mind, after two years in prison, but, perhaps, it is too early. As
for now, I seem to be able to establish only this point: that I feel
like a survivor, in all its meanings. In order to better explain
this, I must rely on a bit of a complex comparison: it is said that
the sea is always motionless at more than 30 meters of depth.
Well, I am sunk to at least 20 meters. That is, I am immersed in
the layer that moves only when some sorts of storms, much
above the norm, are unleashed. But I feel as if I am sinking more
and more, and I can lucidly see the moment when I will reach,
through imperceptible lines, the layer of absolute immobility,
from where it will not be possible even to see the upper layers'

movement, even as a mere sea storm's foamy embroidery. (LC, pp. 217, 218)

On the other hand, will, no matter how extraordinary, is not enough to reconnect the "torn threads" of one's own emotional relationships. If in the past "I was almost proud of my isolation, now I feel all the meanness, lack of feeling, and narrow-mindedness of a life lived exclusively by the will" (LC, pp. 439, 440).

Even his family's pitiful reticence and innocent lies, intended not to increase anxiety, became magnified in the solitude of segregation; they were transformed, in Gramsci's mind, into genuine "conspiracies" to harm him. Of his mother's death, kept hidden from him for a long time, he would write to Julia in 1936:

> Did you think that I did not feel, since 1932, that my poor mother was dead? It was at that time that I felt the strongest pain, and in a truly violent way, although I was seriously debilitated. How could I imagine that my mother, alive, would not write to me or would not have had someone do it for her, and that letters from home would not mention her anymore? I think that false piety is nothing but foolishness and that under the conditions in which a prisoner finds himself it becomes real cruelty, because it creates distrust and the pathological suspicion that who knows what is being kept from him. (LC, pp. 792–793)

In February 1933, he went so far as to suppose that he had been convicted by a very large "organism," of which the special tribunal was only the "external and material appearance."

Among those who had indicted him was also, unconsciously, his wife, but "there are a number of other less unconscious individuals" (LC, p. 690).

It was his relationship with Julia that suffered the consequences of misunderstandings and ambiguities to an exasperating degree. Gramsci learned at the end of 1933 that his wife's precarious mental condition was rapidly deteriorating. "Our letters are a series of 'monologues' that do not always accord with each other" (LC, p. 358). Nor could an effective "dialogue" be established. Gramsci tried hard to take part in the drama that was unfolding in Moscow. He kept himself informed. Through some interesting letters on psychoanalytical theory, he asked and gave advice on the most appropriate treatments for Julia's disease. Yet moments of solidarity, concern, and renewed tenderness alternated with rough periods of coldness and misunderstanding. In November 1932, Gramsci even revealed to Tatiana his decision to break off all contact with his wife, "unilaterally creating a fait accompli":

> I think that Julia, although no longer a young girl, can still be free to start a new life. . . . I will go back into my "Sardinian" shell. I cannot say that I will not suffer, but with every passing day I become more and more desensitized and adaptable. I could bear it. I could adapt. (LC, p. 638)

Gramsci was aware that his own personality was crumbling. It was actually splitting: "one side observes the process, the other undergoes it." The point of no return was near, where "the whole personality will be swallowed by a new 'individual' with impulses, initiatives, and ways of thinking different from the previous ones." The sense of collapse that looms threateningly is expressed in the following excruciating metaphor:

> Imagine a shipwreck and that a certain number of people take refuge in a dinghy to save themselves without knowing where, when, and after what sort of vicissitudes they will actually save themselves. Before the sinking, as is natural, none of the future shipwreck victims thought they would become . . . shipwrecked, and, therefore, much less did they think of being led to commit acts that some survivors, under certain conditions, may commit, for example, the act of becoming . . . a cannibal. Each of them,

after having regained their senses, if questioned about what he would have chosen between facing death and becoming a cannibal, would have answered in utmost good faith that, given the alternative, he would have certainly chosen to die. A shipwreck happens, the refuge in the dinghy, etc. After some days without food, the idea of cannibalism appears in a different light, until, at a certain point, some of those individuals truly become cannibals. But, are they, in reality, the same people? Between the two moments, one in which the alternative is a purely theoretical hypothesis and the other in which the alternative appears in all the strength of immediate need, a "molecular" transformation process has rapidly taken place, in which people are no longer the same before and after. We cannot say . . . that they are the same people. (LC, pp. 692–693)

5. "We must snatch from prison the living and not the dead."

An appeal submitted by Tatiana to the head of the government in September 1932 was finally accepted the February of the following year. The application was filed in order to allow Gramsci to be visited by his personal doctor. On March 20, 1933, Professor Umberto Arcangeli stated, following a medical visit:

Antonio Gramsci, detained at Turi, suffers from Pott's disease; he has tubercular lesions in the upper lobe of the right lung that have led to two hemoptyses, one of which, of considerable amount, was followed by a strong fever lasting several days. He is affected by arteriosclerosis and hypertension. He has fainted multiple times with loss of consciousness and many days of paraphasia. Since October 1932, he has lost seven kilos; he suffers from insomnia and *is no longer able to write as in the past* [italics in original].

In considering such a gloomy diagnosis, one cannot but think of the heroic determination that spurred Gramsci's research in prison. From the pages of the *Notebooks*, the mind of this man appears disconnected from the agony of his body. Any reference to his plight is virtually absent. Those notes could well have been written down under a state of unfettered will and intellect. The exceptional nature of his correspondence fully demonstrates Gramsci the thinker "in flesh and bones." This can be seen in the letters where from a minute description of the symptoms of his disease and drug doses he shifts to a lucid examination of the historical and theoretical reasons for Gentile's break with Croce and for the political phenomenon of "transformism" in Italy (LC, pp. 584–587).

Arcangeli's medical certificate ended with this assessment: "Gramsci cannot survive for long in his actual condition. I consider it necessary for him to be transferred to a civil hospital or clinic, unless he can be granted conditional freedom." In the spring, this was published in France in *L'Humanité* [Humanity] and in *Soccorso Rosso* [Red Rescue]. In Paris, a committee was formed to fight for the release of Gramsci and other persecuted antifascists. Among the members were Rolland and Barbousse. A far-reaching international solidarity campaign also began. From some quarters it was feared that the action might have negative consequences. Togliatti and Sraffa also feared possible retaliation by the regime. However, public opinion cannot be discounted as shaping successive developments in Gramsci's imprisonment.

In the meantime, through a petition submitted in July, Tatiana succeeded in obtaining Gramsci's transfer to the infirmary of another prison. The petition was accepted in October. On November 19, Gramsci left Turi and was provisionally assigned to the infirmary of Civitavecchia prison.

In January 1936, he confided to Julia:

What a terrible impression I felt on the train, after having seen the same roofs for six years, the same walls, the same grim faces,

and to see that during this time the whole wide world had continued to exist with its meadows, its woods, its common people,
the crowds of young people, certain trees and certain vegetable
gardens, but especially what impression I had in looking at
myself in the mirror after so long. I returned immediately near
the *carabinieri.* (LC, p. 772)

On December 7, 1933, he was admitted to Doctor
Cusimano's clinic at Formia in a state of detention. His room windows were barred. He was guarded by a *carabiniere*, while some
others watched over the halls and the garden. "He is gradually
gaining courage again so that we can hope for some improvement
in his physical condition." This would turn out to be Tatiana's
pitiful illusion: Gramsci's condition was desperate. The inadequate treatment he received could not halt the "progressive and
torturing destruction of his physical and psychological state"
(LC, p. 826). These were Gramsci's own words, included in his
request for parole forwarded to Mussolini in October 1934. Too
much time had been lost. He resumed his studies and at times he
set out to write. He tried to resume his correspondence with Julia
and his children, but the reality is expressed in this meager sentence published in *Avanti!*: "We must snatch from prison the living and not the dead."

Having gained conditional freedom, he left the Cusimano
clinic on August 24, 1935, and was admitted to the Quisisana
clinic in Rome. In April 1937, Gramsci regained full freedom. On
April 25, he suffered a cerebral haemorrhage. Gramsci died two
days later. He was forty-six years old.

6. His Relationship with the Party during His Prison Years

There is no political correspondence in *Letters from Prison.*
During the trial in Rome, Gramsci had followed a common line

with the other defendants. They admitted to being active members of the Communist Party, but denied holding managerial posts and carrying out managerial functions. Naturally suspicious, aware of meticulous prison control, Gramsci regularly avoided exchanging letters with his party's comrades, either in a direct or encrypted form. It is therefore not simple to determine what sort of relationship he had with the Italian Communist Party leadership, which had emigrated abroad, and with the militants and leaders who had been arrested. However, from some sections of the *Notebooks* it can be deduced that those relationships had been substantially altered, seeing how he dealt with political problems occurring during the decade in which he was cut off from any possible immediate interventions and initiatives. We reach the same conclusion when reading the statements of those who had the opportunity of speaking with him during his detention.

It is certainly known that Gramsci disagreed with the "turn" in the Communist International, which the Italian Communist Party followed. In 1928–29 the Comintern, having abandoned the "single front" strategy, considered the relative stabilization of capitalism to have reached its end and that a new revolutionary situation was imminent. The theory of "social-fascism" identified social democracy as the most advanced element of reaction, a simple variant of fascism. In 1930, at Turi, while talking about politics with his fellow inmates during recess, Gramsci had stressed the need for an intermediate "democratic" phase.

It is true that Gramsci's perspective on politics, at least since the "turn," diverged from that of the Communist leadership. However, there is no indication that Gramsci broke with the party or that he was expelled from it. His connection to the party's Central Committee abroad, mainly through Sraffa, never ceased. On the contrary, it would be Gramsci himself who would increasingly express his political discomfort. Historiographic research and the finding of key documents dispel any notion of any "diabolical plan" set against him. This is especially important with reference to a letter from Ruggero Grieco dated February 10, 1928, which aroused a nagging suspicion in the prisoner that some of the exiled leaders intended to worsen his position, in view of the beginning of the trial.

On April 30, Gramsci wrote to Julia in this regard:

I recently received . . . a strange letter signed by Ruggero that asked for an answer. Perhaps my life in jail made me more suspicious than required by normal wisdom. But the fact is that this letter, in spite of its stamp and postmark, has ticked me off. (LC, p. 186)

He returned more directly to this issue in December 1932, in a letter to Tatiana:

You remember, in 1928, when I was in prison in Milan [San Vittore], I received a letter from a "friend" abroad. You remember that I told you about this very strange letter and that the judge, after handing it to me, literally added these words: "Honorable Gramsci, you certainly have some friends who wish you a lengthy jail sentence." You yourself referred to this letter with a judgment that ended with the adjective "criminal." Well, this letter was extremely "affectionate" toward me; it appeared to be written by someone eager to "comfort me," giving me courage, and so on. Yet both the judge's opinion and the one that you referred to me were objectively correct. . . . In reading some lines in the letter, the judge pointed out to me that (apart from the rest) the letter could have been an immediate catastrophe for me. And this was not only because there was no wish to worsen the situation and it was preferable to just let it go. Was it a wicked act or an irresponsible imprudence? It is difficult to say. It could be both; it is possible that the one who wrote this letter was irresponsibly stupid and someone else, a less stupid one, had induced him to write the letter. (LC, pp. 646–647)

What was the content of this "charged" letter? Grieco wanted to inform Gramsci about the development of internal strife in the Russian party, which culminated in November 1927 with the expulsion of Trotsky and Zinoviev, and about the opinion of the political office of the Italian Communist Party, in agreement with the Bolshevik majority. The subtle content of the news and the confidential tone of the letter betrayed Grieco's interlocutor to be a high-ranking Communist leader. But, really, were not the fascist police already aware of this? Gramsci was well known to police (*Pubblica sicurezza*) as secretary of the party's executive since 1924. It is not even clear that the letter was ever used as evidence by the prosecution during his trial.

In order to dismantle the hypothesis of a "plot," two more letters—very similar to the one sent to Gramsci—were posted the same day by Grieco to Scoccimarro and Terracini. The latter was answered in March without any consequence. Even though he had been in the same predicament as Gramsci, Terracini never suspected any devious machinations and hidden hostility.

Gramsci's obsessive doubt was communicated to Tatiana, who insisted, even after her brother-in-law's death, on finding out the truth about this supposed plot. Sraffa's opinion on this matter is very interesting and measured. In a letter from September 1937, he wrote to his girlfriend explaining a banal misunderstanding:

> The matter has been clarified. But suppose we couldn't freely write each other, that you would have been in terrible physical and mental condition for ten years, alone with your own ideas, your misunderstanding would have grown in your mind. . . . I am convinced that something similar (obviously, in a more serious context) happened in the case of Nino's notorious letter. To me, reading it with an aloof mind, it is clear that it was a writer's imprudence, but there was no "malice" and much less any dia-

bolical plan. I was reassured in my opinion by the fact that Nino said that he became suspicious because of the judge's comments; and we all know that to instill such suspicions is typical of a judge's profession. (LTG, pp. 187–188)

And it would be Ruggero Grieco himself, on the first anniversary of Gramsci's death, who would write to Julia on behalf of the party's Central Committee:

Our duty now is to publish the main writings of our Leader, and it is to this task that we want now to devote ourselves. Thus the teachings of this great Italian Communist will be available to all workers and progressive men in our country ("*Ruggero Grieco a Giulia Schucht.*" [Ruggero Grieco to Julia Schucht], LN, p. 105)

The *Prison Notebooks*

1. "A laboratory of ideas."

One of Gramsci's prison companions recalled that on the eve of his transfer from Turi prison:

> we went to the warehouse to prepare his luggage, accompanied by the prison guard in charge. While, in agreement with me, he kept the guard engaged with small talk, I put the 18 handwritten notebooks in the trunk with other stuff.

In reality, there were twenty-one notebooks. Between February 1922 and the last few months of 1933, with clear and thin handwriting, Gramsci filled seventeen notebooks with annotations on various topics. Four others were filled with translation exercises from two languages he deemed of particular importance, German and Russian. During his Formia period (December 1933–August 1935), he completed another twelve notebooks.

Thus, the total number of prison notebooks was thirty-three, containing more than two thousand annotations preceded by a section paragraph sign (§) and often by title.

It was Gramsci's wish that his own manuscripts be delivered to Julia. Tatiana told Sraffa about this on May 12, 1937, asking him, among other things, whether he was willing to put them in order: "There is no doubt that this work should be done by a competent person, not otherwise" (LC, p. 260). However, Sraffa had a different opinion. Knowing what value was attributed to Gramsci's literary legacy by Communist Party leaders, he advised Tatiana to send the notebooks immediately to Moscow. "I am convinced," he wrote to her in September 1937, "that you should send this stuff immediately, without delay" (LTG, p. 186). However the shipping would be postponed by a year. Gramsci's manuscripts arrived in the Soviet Union in July 1938. They were delivered to the Italian representative of the Comintern. Palmiro Togliatti was in Spain, where civil war had broken out in the summer of 1936, instigated by a group of generals headed by future dictator Francisco Franco. After receiving the first copies in Barcelona, under constant bombardment by fascist airplanes, Togliatti began the task of editing the notebooks by candlelight with some collaborators. The aim was to prepare the work for immediate publication. The initiative would be hampered, however, by the Spanish tragedy, the outbreak of World War II, and Togliatti's arrest.

The first edition of the *Prison Notebooks* appeared between 1948 and 1951 published by Einaudi Editore. Gramsci's annotations were grouped according to themes and topics, in six separate volumes, under editorial titles that have become well known:

- *Historical Materialism and the Philosophy of Benedetto Croce* (1948)
- *Intellectuals and Cultural Organization* (1949)
- *The Risorgimento* (1949)
- *Notes on Machiavelli, Politics, and the Modern State* (1949)

- *National Literature and Life* (1950)
- *Past and Present* (1951)

The spread of the thematic edition of the *Prison Notebooks* has been tremendous but disputes about the correctness and legitimacy of the criteria chosen for the publication have not been lacking. It can nevertheless be said that other options would have hardly ensured such a wide circulation of Gramscian thought. The fragmentary state of the notes and the author's attempt to rework and reorganize them progressively into homogenous groups all seemed to justify the choices made by the early editors of the work.

Through the years, it was the great interest aroused by these texts that led to the preparation of a critical edition of the *Prison Notebooks* in 1975, again through Einaudi Editore. It consists of three large volumes, more than a quarter of which are comprised of notes and appendices. The notebooks are arranged in chronological order, exactly the way Gramsci had compiled them.

The critical edition turned out to be a precious instrument for Gramscian scholars, and put the inevitable philological limits of the preceding thematic volumes into focus. However, it is not an easy work to read. The older edition of Gramscian anthologies remains all the more useful at least insofar as it depicts an earlier approach and a layperson's study of the *Prison Notebooks.*

The chronological order of Gramsci's prison notes makes for a clear display of his working method. To begin with, it is clear that he often worked contemporaneously on different notebooks or returned to previous ones to add new notes on the blank pages he had left behind. If it was possible, therefore, to date the beginning of each notebook with certainty, it is sometimes very difficult to do so for passages from one notebook to another and for forward and backward references. This problem specifically relates to the so-called "miscellaneous" notebooks, that is, those in which Gramsci gathered reading notes and scattered observations, transcribed other authors' passages, and so on. During a second editing phase, such material was sometimes grouped according to topics in "special" notebooks, as Gramsci defined them. In the critical edition the texts have been dileneated as follows:

- Texts A, those from the first draft, used again in other notes, with major or minor variants, above all in "special" notebooks;
- Texts B, those appearing as a single draft;
- Texts C, those appearing as a second draft.

All these elements may appear to be more or less unnecessary technical details but they are indispensable in order to introduce some fundamental characteristics of the *Prison Notebooks*. The unitary inspiration of Gramsci's work, the leitmotif discussed in the introduction of this book, is actually not self-evident. The drafting of the prison notes is predominantly of a temporary nature and is beset by a sense of incompleteness. They offer a vast laboratory of ideas, where all the preparatory material is stored for the writing of a series of essays, according to a plan worked out in several stages. These essays were never written. Gramsci's intellectual itinerary, anchored to a human and political vicissitude strongly lived and suffered, has nothing in common with that of a "quiet bookworm that feeds itself with old printed paper and writes dissertations on the use of the imperfect tense in *Sicco Polenton*" (LC, p. 329).[1] The reader of the *Prison Notebooks* needs to constantly keep this in mind. He is not dealing with a final work that can perhaps be taken in passively. There are more open questions than certainties and truths. But it is exactly the anti-dogmatic and critical characteristics of the *Prison Notebooks* that offer a lesson in method that is always current.

2. Ideology and "the philosophy of praxis."

In the *Prison Notebooks*, Gramsci frequently referred to his journalistic activity, which kept him busy from his youth to his arrest. "Journalism" is the title of a "special" notebook of 1934, to which he also devoted various other scattered notes. In one of these, Gramsci mentioned "*Brevi cenni sull'universo*" [A Brief Survey on the Universe] as a "caricature of a pedantic and pretentious title" (Q, pp. 1029–1030). This witty motto is worth remembering when treating Gramsci's rich and articulated theoretical universe in a few pages.

Many interpretative categories, as well as Gramsci's simple expressions, have become part of everyday language in Italy. One could also say, using a typical Gramscian notion, that they have become "common sense."

The concept of common sense is viewed by Gramsci as "ambiguous, contradictory, and multifaceted" (Q, p. 1399). Yet it is of noticeable importance. "What is exactly the virtue of this so-called 'common sense' or 'good sense'?" The most immediate answer is that "common sense identifies exact, simple, and practical causes through a set of judgments, and it does not allow itself to be drawn into metaphysical, pseudo-profound, pseudo-scientific, etc., quibbles and absurdities" (Q, p. 1334). But common sense is also "conservative" and "pettily misoneistic." In other words, it is contrary to innovation. It cannot be used as "the proof of the truth" of a theory. However, if a theory manages to become accepted as common sense it means that "it has a considerable expansionary and evidentiary force" (Q, p. 1400). Hence, every philosophy tends to become common sense and to impose itself not only among small groups of intellectuals, but also among popular strata.

What is the intellectual position of the common man?

He has formed views, convictions, discriminating criteria, and norms of behavior. Every supporter of a viewpoint that contrasts

with his own, being intellectually superior, knows how to argue
his reasons more than a common man can do; he is able to over-
whelm him with logic, and so on. Should common man, therefore, change his convictions? Why can he not assert himself in
the immediacy of debate? But, then, he might have to change his
mind everyday, that is, whenever he faces an ideological opponent that exceeds him intellectually. What then underpins his
philosophy, especially the form of philosophy that he considers
more important than the standard of conduct? The most important element is, indeed, of a non-rational nature; it is one of faith.
But in whom and in what? Especially in the social group to
which he belongs, insofar as it largely thinks the same way as he
does. Common man thinks that the many cannot go wrong, in
contrast to what the opponent would have him believe. Even if
he himself is, in truth, incapable of sustaining and articulating
his own opinions as his opponent does, he is certain that there
is in his group someone who knows how to do it, certainly even
better than that particular opponent. In fact, he remembers having heard the reasons for his faith expounded widely and coher-
ently, such that he has remained convinced. (Q, p. 1391)

To win large sections of people over to new ideas, it is necessary to start from a critique of old common sense, which also
extends to "individual" philosophies, systems of thought elaborated by specialists that were at the origin of the history of philosophy in its proper sense. By analyzing common sense, which
Gramsci also defined as the "folklore of philosophy," since "it is
always in between folklore proper" and "the scientists' philosophy, science, and economics" (Q, p. 2271), it can be concluded
that "all men are philosophers." This is not a demagogical formula intended to flatter the masses. On the contrary, Gramsci
was very strict in keeping the field of specialized culture distinct
from improvisation and amateurism. One has only to read the
following passage:

If a guy, who never studied Chinese and knows only his province's dialect [in Italy], is asked to translate a Chinese passage, he will be reasonably perplexed. At first, he will take it as a joke, but, if one insists, he will think he is made fun of, so he will be offended and start fighting. And yet the same guy, without being solicited, will think he is authorized to speak about all sorts of topics that he knows just as well as Chinese, about which he knows not the technical language, the historical context, the relationship to other topics, and sometimes their distinctive traits. (Q, p. 1779)

What does it mean, then, that *everybody* is a philosopher? It means nothing more than that in practical life—in the "practical activity" of men—"there is an implicit concept of the world, a philosophy" (Q, p. 1255). Between professional philosophers and those who carry out other activities there is a "quantitative" difference, not a "qualitative" one:

The professional philosopher or technician not only "thinks" with more logical rigor and more consistency, with a greater feel of the systematic than other men, but he knows the entire history of thought, that is, he can come to terms with the development of thought up to his time. (Q, p. 1342)

In the field of thought, he serves the same function as other specialists in various scientific fields. However, there is a difference:

The specialist philosopher is closer to other men than other specialists . . . one cannot think of any man without thinking that he is also a philosopher, who thinks, precisely because thinking is proper of man as such (unless he is a pathological idiot). (Q, pp. 1342–1343)

Or, stated in more general terms, "one cannot talk of non-intellectuals, because they do not exist. . . . There is no human activity that excludes intellectual intervention" (Q, p. 1550). Nevertheless, can a man who fries two eggs or mends his jacket be called a cook or tailor? Certainly not. Similarly, not everybody has intellectual functions in a society. Historically, there have emerged "groups whose role is to specialize in the exercise of the intellect" (Q, p. 1516). These social categories are especially tied to dominant social groups:

> One of the most important characteristics of every group that increases its power is its fight to assimilate and conquer traditional intellectuals "ideologically." This occurs much more rapidly and effectively inasmuch as the given group simultaneously develops its own organic intellectuals. (Q, p. 1517)

Gramsci did not underestimate the historical role of traditional intellectuals. It is therefore necessary to come to terms with "individual" philosophers like Benedetto Croce, the "secular pope" of national culture. Echoing Engels's *Anti-Dühring*, Gramsci maintained that writing an *Anti-Croce* "would be worth ten years of activity by a whole group of men" (Q, p. 1234). The history of philosophy, in Gramsci's view, is not exhausted in the "philosophers' philosophy." This is the story:

> of attempts and ideological initiatives by a certain class of individuals to change, correct, and further improve existing concepts of the world in any given time, and, therefore, to change the rules of behavior that conform and relate to them, that is, to change practices as a whole.

At this point, Gramsci draws attention to other aspects of the history of philosophy: the different ideas of the world in the masses and limited circles of intellectuals, and the nexus between these various cultural entities and philosophical tradition *sensu stricto*:

> The philosophy of a historical period is not the philosophy of one philosopher or another, one or another group of intellectuals or one or another large part of the masses. It is a combination of all these elements that culminates in a certain direction. Its very same culmination becomes the norm of collective action, that is, it becomes concrete and complete (integral) history. The philosophy of a historical period is nothing more than the "history" of that period. It is nothing more than the mass of variations that the leading group was able to determine in the previous reality. In this sense, history and philosophy are inseparable. They form a "bloc." (Q, p. 1255)

The subjects of history, the true protagonists of the present cultural and political "bloc," are the masses. The great intellectual must then "throw himself, too, into practical life, and become an organizer of the practical aspects of culture ... he must democratize himself" (Q, p. 689). The historical personality of an "individual" philosopher is no longer defined on the basis of new truisms or original discoveries that remain the patrimony of small groups. A philosopher's personality is no longer "limited to his own physical self, but it is an active social relation of the cultural environment" (Q, p. 1332). This new type of philosopher, formed historically, is called the "democratic philosopher" by Gramsci. Modern educational principles, according to which the relationship between teacher and pupil is reciprocal, that is, "every teacher is a pupil, and every pupil is a teacher," is not only about the school environment. All social elements influence each other reciprocally, individuals among themselves, intellectuals and non-intellectuals as well as rulers and subjects. Now, the cultural environment where the philosopher operates acts on him as well. It functions as a "master" and forces him into "continuous self-criticism" (Q, p. 1331).

The source of Gramsci's elaboration was Marx's theory, specifically the third of the eleven theses on the German philosopher Ludwig Feuerbach, written by Marx in 1845. The *Theses on Feuerbach*, which Gramsci translated while in prison, are collected in the Appendix to the critical edition of the *Prison Notebooks*. With respect to the third thesis, one reads:

> The materialistic doctrine by which men are the products of environment and education, and that, therefore, changes in men are the products of another environment and a different education, overlooks the fact that it is precisely the environment that is modified by men and that the educator himself must be educated. (Q, p. 2356)

Marx's *Theses on Feuerbach* includes a very well known motto almost ubiquitous in modern socialist thought. Gramsci's translation of the last of the *Theses* is rendered thus: "Philosophers have only interpreted the world in different ways; now it is about changing it" (Q, p. 2357). Is this a "gesture of rejection of philosophy of every sort" on Marx's part? In Gramsci's view:

> Even if one were to hold the absurd assumption that Marx intended to "supplant" philosophy in general with practical activity, one would have to "unsheath" the peremptory argument that you cannot deny philosophy if not by philosophizing, that is, by reaffirming what you have denied.

Marx expressed his annoyance with respect to a certain way of philosophizing akin to parroting. However, his real purpose was "the energetic affirmation of the unity of theory and practice" (Q, p. 1270).

The unity of theory and practice is also reaffirmed in another phrase to which Gramsci often referred in the *Prison*

Notebooks. It is the passage that concludes Engels's 1886 essay, *Ludwig Feuerbach and the End of Classical German Philosophy*: "The German workers' movement is heir to German classical philosophy."

In Notebook 10, titled *"La filosofia di Benedetto Croce"* [Benedetto Croce's Philosophy], Gramsci remarked:

> The proposition that the German proletariat is heir to German classical philosophy indeed contains the identity between history and philosophy; in the same manner goes the proposition that philosophers have so far only explained the world and that now it is about changing it. (Q, p. 1241)

The identity of history and philosophy "immanent in historical materialism" was supported by Croce as well. In Croce's understanding, as it was then developing, these ideas were not carried to their logical conclusions. It had remained something different from Marx and Engels's materialistic understanding. It is through the identity of history and philosophy that we come to identify history and politics, and, consequently, to identify politics and philosophy:

> But if it is necessary to admit this identity, how is it still possible to distinguish ideologies (equal to instruments of political action, according to Croce) from philosophy? That is, this distinction will be possible, but only gradually (quantitatively) and not qualitatively. On the contrary, ideologies will become "true" philosophy because they will turn into the "popularization" of philosophy, which brings the masses into concrete actions and the transformation of reality. That is, they will be the aspect of every philosophical idea from the perspective of the masses, which, in the philosopher, assumes the character of abstract universality, outside of time and space, a character peculiar to literary and anti-historical origins. (Q, pp. 1241, 1242)

In Notebook 10, Gramsci also conceded that just because "the concept of unity of theory and practice and that of philosophy and politics was not clear to me," he had been in years past "tendentiously mostly Crocean" (Q, p. 1233). As proof of his youthful Croceanism, Gramsci recalled a passage in his *Città futura* that preceded Croce's piece on religion. It was 1937. With the passing of time, his dialogue with Croce did not end, but the points of theoretical departure multiplied and became more pronounced. Also, the Neapolitan philosopher's attitude regarding fascism would exacerbate such elements of discord so as to provoke fierce criticism. As a case in point, one can read in the *Notebooks* a wisecrack about the connections of Croce (and Gentile) with "Senators Agnelli and Benni" being stronger than those with Aristotle and Plato (Q, p. 1515).

Irrespective of this, Gramsci never denied Croce's influence, nor the progressive function, in Italian culture, of the "religion of freedom" spread by the latter. One can rather say that the closer Gramsci approached Marx, the more his intellectual path diverged from that of Croce.

His article *"La rivoluzione contro il 'Capitale'"* [The Revolution Against "Capital"] appeared in the same year as *Città futura* [City of the Future]. It was previously considered a typical example of how Gramsci's thought differs from that of Marx. This was evidenced by a passage from the Preface to *Per la critica dell' economia politica* [For a Critique of Political Economy]. It is significant that in Notebook 13, while discussing the political problem of "relations of power," Gramsci sets two fundamental points of his own analysis in relation to a passage from the same preface:

> It is the problem of the relation between structure and super-
> structure that needs to be formulated and solved in order to ana-
> lyze correctly the forces that operate in a given historical period
> and determine their relationship. We must operate within the

framework of two principles: 1) that no society poses itself certain tasks unless necessary and sufficient conditions for their solution do not already exist or are not at least materializing and developing; 2) that no society can be dissolved and substituted by another until all the forms of life implicit in its social relations have been completely unfolded. (Q, pp. 1578–1579)

The terms are almost identical to Marx's. His rethinking is radical in relation to the "voluntarism," and, in general, to the idealistic positions of the early years of his political commitment. Gramsci's rethinking followed his in-depth study of Marxist classics, and, above all, the political experience acquired during the decisive years for the history of the socialist movement. The problem of working class defeat in the West and its success in the East occupied most of Gramsci's time in prison. Having been the head of the Communist Party and an active participant in Turin's mass proletarian movement put Gramsci in a position unique among Marxist thinkers to unify theory and practice, thought and action. These experiences have certainly weighed considerably on Gramsci's novel contributions to Marxist theory. He is a "concrete philosopher" who does not limit himself to argue about the world but works to change it by means of political action. In this sense, he appears to be a strict follower of Marx. But was Gramsci really an orthodox Marxist?

In Notebook 11, he wrote about the concept of orthodoxy in relation to the "philosophy of praxis" (this expression was adopted usually in reference to historical materialism, and sometimes Marxism in general, in order to protect himself from prison censorship):

Orthodoxy is not to be sought in this or that follower of philosophy of praxis, in this or that tendency connected to doctrines foreign to the original one, but in the fundamental concept that

philosophy of praxis is "self-contained." It contains in itself all
the fundamental elements to build not only a total and integral
world concept, a complete philosophy and theory of the natural
sciences, but also to bring to life an integral practical organization of society, that is, to become a complete and integral civilization. (Q, p. 1434)

The fact that Marxism is an independent and original philosophy was one of the conclusions of Antonio Labriola's theoretical research. "It is necessary to work in this direction,"
Gramsci asserted, "pursuing and developing Labriola's position" (Q, p. 422).

The defense of the autonomy of Marxist understandings of
the world is an important aspect of Gramsci's orthodoxy. Not that
he considered comparisons with other scientific doctrines and
disciplines of different orientation of little use or even useless or
damaging. Some attempts at integrating Marxism, to combine its
principles with those of other philosophies, have turned out to be
"abject and vile opportunism" (Q, p. 1435), in terms of an inabil-
ity to cut ties with old ways of thinking and acting. Nevertheless,
a Marxist's attitude must be "always critical and never dogmatic"
(Q, p. 425). This was Marx's real teaching anyway. Gramsci's
polemic against those scholars that were busy transforming historical materialism into eternal and absolute truth was mordant.
The main target in the *Notebooks* was Nikolai I. Bukharin's book,
Historical Materialism: A System of Sociology, first published in
Moscow in 1921. Gramsci's opposition to Bukharin's thesis was
absolute, although he had used the book in 1925 seemingly without critical reservations in handouts written for the party's
school. On philosophical grounds, Gramsci rejected Bukharin's
"ultra-materialistic" position:

For a philosophy of praxis, "matter" must be understood neither
in the meaning taken from the natural sciences (physics, chem-

istry, mechanics, etc.), nor the one taken from materialist meta-physics. Different physical properties (chemical, mechanical, etc.), which together form matter, are only taken into account insofar as they become a productive "economic element." Thus, matter is not to be considered as such, but as historically and socially organized for production. (Q, p. 1442)

In Bukharin's system, philosophical materialism is treated as *real* philosophy and the philosophy of praxis is simply *sociology*. "What is the true meaning of this assertion?" Gramsci asked himself:

If it were true, the theory of philosophy of praxis would be philosophical materialism. But in that case, what does it mean that philosophy of praxis is sociology? And what would this sociology be? A science of politics and historiography? Or a systematic collection, classified according to a certain order, of purely empirical observations of the art of politics and of the external canons of historical research? (Q, pp. 1431–1432)

This reduction of philosophy of praxis to sociology means the understanding of the world is reduced to a "mechanical form that gives the impression of having all of history in one's pocket" (Q, p. 1428). Mechanization, the absence of dialectical spirit, and historical and political determinism are the results of Bukharin's dogmatic Marxism. With the expression "historical materialism" more weight is given to the term "materialism," while in Gramsci's view it should be the opposite, since Marx is essentially a "historicist" (Q, p. 433). The nexus between the economic structure of society and the ideological and juridical superstructures is not automatic and unilateral: superstructures are not pure and simple reflexes of material relationships. Gramsci fought bitterly against so-called "economism," that distorted view for which the structure looked like a "hidden god" that creates and rules every social manifestation and mechanism.

What is the reason that a critical doctrine such as Marx's can be transformed into an infallible system, one that is self-referential, almost a theology? The theoretical assumption of the philosophy of praxis, by which every eternal and absolute truth is of practical origins, represents a transitional value that will be judged by history and is valid for Marxism as well. And yet it is difficult to explain it "without shaking those convictions necessary for action." From these difficulties it became clear that "the same philosophy of praxis tends to become *ideology* in the negative sense, that is, a dogmatic system of absolute and eternal truth" (Q, p. 1489).

But what is ideology? What is the function of ideological superstructures in the historical unfolding of humanity? At this point it is useful to read the entire paragraph of Notebook 7, appropriately titled "Ideologies":

> An error in estimating the importance of ideology is, I think, due to the fact (not by chance) that the term is used to indicate both a certain superstructure necessary to a certain structure and the arbitrary cogitations of some individuals. The negative sense of the word has spread to the point that it has changed and denatured the theoretical analysis of the term. The process of this mistake can be easily reconstructed: 1) ideology is identified as distinct from structure and it is asserted that it is not ideologies that changed structure, but vice versa; 2) it is asserted that a certain political solution is "ideological," that is, it is insufficient to change structure, while in thinking that this can occur, it is asserted that it is useless, stupid, etc.; 3) it is then asserted that every ideology is "pure" appearance, useless, stupid, etc.
>
> At this point, we must distinguish between historically organic ideologies, which are necessary to a certain structure, and arbitrary ideologies, rationalistic and "intended." Being historically necessary, their validity is of a "psychological" nature; they "organize" human masses, shape the ground on which men

act and become aware of their position, fight, and so on. Being "arbitrary," they create nothing but "movements," polemics, etc.; (the latter are not even completely useless either, because they are like the error that is counterpoised to a truth that asserts it). (Q, pp. 868–869)

Further on in Notebook 7, in a comment entitled *Validità delle ideologie* [The Validity of Ideologies], Gramsci recalled, by heart, Marx's statement that "popular persuasion is often as strong as material force" (Q, p. 869). Obviously, he was referring to Marx's early essay *A Contribution to the Critique of Hegel's Philosophy of Right*, where one reads that "even theory transforms itself into a material force as soon as it penetrates the masses." Therefore, it is through Marx that Gramsci premised his idea of an "historical bloc," in the set of economic structure and ideological superstructures:

material forces are the content and ideologies are the form, a merely didactic distinction of form and content, because material forces could not possibly be historically conceived without form, and ideologies would be individual whims without material forces. (Ibid.)

Finally, Gramsci's comprehensive theoretical analysis is based on the "necessary reciprocity between structure and superstructure (a reciprocity that is precisely the real dialectical process)" (Q, p. 1052).

The historical and political importance that Gramsci entrusted to the function of intellectuals and cultural organization did not depend on the persistency of idealistic components in his thought. He does not deny that "in the final analysis" structure is the defining element in the formation of ideologies and social contrasts. But men become aware, as Marx also considered, of the same "conflicts of structure in the field of ideology" (Q, p. 1249).

Only on the basis of dogmatic and economistic premises is it possible to deem ideologies as illusory appearances, deprived of any effective sense.

For a philosophy of praxis, ideologies, besides being real historical facts, are powerful tools of political rule. They must be known, understood, and resisted for specific political reasons: "to make the governed intellectually independent of rulers, to destroy one hegemonic entity to create another one" (Q, p. 1319). The philosophy of praxis considers superstructures an "objective and functioning" reality. Like any other philosophy, materialistic concepts of history are also a superstructure, but with a fundamental difference:

> Other ideologies are inorganic creations because contradictory in character, and because they are intended to reconcile opposed and contradictory interests. Their "historicism" will be short-lived because contradiction emerges after every event of which they were the instrument. The philosophy of praxis, instead, does not tend to resolve existing contradictions peacefully in history and society. On the contrary, it is the same theory of these contradictions. It is not an instrument of rule for the dominant classes to gain the consent, of and exercise hegemony over, the subordinate classes. It is the expression of these subordinate classes who want to educate themselves in the art of governing and are interested in knowing all truths, even unpleasant ones, and to avoid (impossible) deceptions by the upper class, so much higher than themselves. (Q, pp. 1319, 1320)

3. Politics: Hegemony and Party

Gramscian ideas of hegemony are rooted in the analysis of the historic bloc, where the true reciprocal influence of structure and superstructure are manifested, in the critique of the science of economics, of political mechanistics and theoretical dogmatism. Gramsci's reading of Marx is clearly distinguishable from the vulgar simplifications that were established in the Communist International. The transition from "political society" to "regulated society," that is, the overcoming of the "concept of necessity" by the "concept of freedom," is based on Marx's philosophy. Marx's understanding of the world, having become the "theory of a class," would eventually "become a State." This process had materialized through Lenin, about which Gramsci highlights the importance of the "concept and the fact of hegemony" (Q, p. 882). The Russian revolutionary succeeded in advancing Marxism not only in his political theory, but also in his philosophy. On the one hand, he showed the possibility of "realizing" Marx's philosophy; on the other, he was the first to understand that this realization, i.e., the affirmation of the subordinate classes, had to come to terms with cultural and ideational struggle.

To establish a "planned society," characterized by the identity of the individual and the state, it is necessary to have a solid cultural project. Destroying past social relations is just as difficult as creating new ones. In fact, it is not about "destroying material things, but invisible and impalpable 'relations,' even if they hide in material things" (Q, p. 708). To be aware of this involves the capacity for developing a very articulated and complex interpretation of history. Nothing could be further from the formula that connects human history with the typical regular processes of natural history. If natural sciences allow, perhaps, the prediction of the evolution of the processes of nature, there is no way to predict society's future. "One knows what has been or what is, and not what will be, which is a 'non-existing,' and therefore unknowable by definition" (Q, p. 1404). It is a gross error to think that communism is the inevitable result of the struggle between the bourgeoisie and the proletariat. Only the struggle can be scientifically predicted, not its forms and results. The subordinate classes aim to achieve political power, but the impetus of economic necessity is not sufficient to fulfill this "historical mission":

> Every historical act cannot but be accomplished by "collective man." That is, it presupposes the achievement of a 'cultural-social' unity by which a variety of differentiated intentions, with heterogeneous purposes, merge into the same purpose on the basis of an (equal) and shared view of the world. (Q, p. 1331)

The philosophy of praxis, in its recent development, claims "the moment of hegemony."

It is essential to valorizing "the cultural front as necessary as those that are merely economic and political" (Q, p. 1224).

The supremacy of a class or a social group does not manifest itself as "domination." In a situation in which the dominant class has only "pure coercive force," there is a "crisis of authority"; namely, that the masses separate themselves from traditional ideologies. The loss of "consent," in fact, determines a critical phase with unpredictable results, in which "the old dies and the new cannot rise" (Q, p. 311). The determining factor of hegemony is, thus, "intellectual and moral direction":

> A social group can and, indeed, must already be a leader before conquering government power (this is one of the main conditions for the same conquest of power); later, when it exercises power and even if it has firm control, it becomes dominant, but it must also continue to be a 'leader'. (Q, pp. 2010, 2011)

Gramsci's great innovation, even compared to Lenin, is pointing out the need to gain "consent" even before the material conquest of power. In Lenin, the principle of hegemony was directly connected to the peculiar historical situation in which he worked. The proletariat, who emerged as the winner in the October Revolution, should guide other social groups, take over the cultural machinery, and exercise ideological leadership in addition to political leadership. It is true that for Gramsci intellectual and moral reform is linked to an economic reform program and the emancipation of the working class. But precisely in order to determine the conditions favorable to a change in the social structure, it is necessary to weaken the bourgeois class in the ideological field. However, "changes in the way of thinking, in beliefs, and in opinions, do not occur in quick and generalized 'explosions'; they usually occur in 'subsequent combinations' according to the most varied 'formulae'" (Q, p. 34). Intellectuals, as organizers of hegemony, have therefore a long task ahead, especially in a period of "war of position."

More than a decade had passed since the Russian Revolution. Furthermore, Gramsci's investigation covered the transition to socialism in an industrially advanced country. In Notebook 6, in a comment titled *Passaggio dalla guerra manovrata (e dall'attacco frontale) alla guerra di posizione anche nel campo politico* [The transition from a maneuvered war (and from frontal attack) to a war of position also in the political field], one can read that this was "the most important political question of the postwar period and the most difficult to be resolved the right way" (Q, p. 801). Objecting to Trotsky, the political theorist of frontal attack, Gramsci held that maneuvered war (or war of movement) exists:

> when it is about the conquest of non-decisive positions and, thus, it is not necessary to mobilize all the resources of hegemony and of the state. But when, for one reason or another, these positions have lost their value and only the decisive ones are important, then we move to siege war, intense, difficult, which requires exceptional patience and an inventive spirit. (Q, p. 802)

The war of position demands enormous sacrifices to enormous masses of the population. It requires a "concentration of unheard-of hegemony." In politics, the war of position, "when it is won, is definitively decisive." In Notebook 7, Gramsci disagrees with Trotsky's "theory of permanent revolution" as reflecting the theory of maneuvered war. In the final analysis, it is intended as a reflection "of the general, economic, cultural, and social conditions of a country where the frameworks of national life are embryonic and freed up" (Q, p. 865). To Gramsci it seemed that Lenin, although he did not have time to expand his formula:

> understood the necessity of changing from a maneuvered war, successfully applied in the East, in 1917, to a war of position, which was the only possible option in the West. In the East, the state was everything; civil society was primordial and gelatinous. In the West, there existed a balanced relationship between state and civil society, and in the trembling of the state, the strength of civil society was immediately evident. The state was only a forward trench, behind which there was a sturdy succession of fortresses and madhouses. (Q, p. 866)

The image of a "trench-State" supported by fortresses and madhouses is a very effective one. The road to power is not simply passing from one dominant group to another in the state machinery. "Direct control" is expressed in the state and in "legal" government. To civil society, instead, corresponds the "function of 'hegemony' that the dominant group exerts over the whole society" (Q, pp. 1518, 1519). It is civil society, which Gramsci placed between economic structure and the state, that "must be radically transformed in a concrete way and not only on legal paper or scientists' books" (Q, pp. 1253, 1254). The political party, as the "collective intellectual," is the main instrument for the transformation necessary to realize a new hegemonic system.

In order to define the political party's characteristics, Gramsci was inspired by Machiavelli's treatise, *The Prince*, written around 1515 and first printed in 1532. This work marks the beginning of modern political science, separating it from morals and religion. In this "living" book, Gramsci wrote, the protagonist, the prince:

> did not exist in historical reality; he was not introduced to the Italian people with the features of objective immediacy, but was a pure doctrinaire abstraction, the symbol of the leader, and the ideal condottiere. (Q, p. 1556)

The "modern prince" cannot but be an "organism" today:

> This organism was already given by history, and it is the political party that is the first cell wherein the germ of the collective will is gathered that tends to become universal and total. (Q, p. 1558)

The power attributed by Gramsci to the working class is impressive:

> The modern Prince, as he develops, upsets the entire system of moral and intellectual relations, since his development means precisely that every act is considered useful or harmful, virtuous or wicked, only insofar as the point of reference is the same modern Prince and is used to increase his power or to contrast it. The Prince, in people's minds, replaces divinity or the categorical imperative, becoming the basis of modern secularism and of the complete secularization of all life and all customary relations. (Q, p. 1561)

This all-encompassing understanding of the party originated from the historical contingency in which Gramsci's thought developed. It is in contrast with a totalitarian and repressive regime that gives way only to frontal conflict, to the competition between hegemonies "armored with coercion." To conquer democracy, "it can be necessary—in fact, it is almost always necessary—to have a strongly centralized party" (Q, p. 236). Nevertheless, Gramsci did

not refrain from denouncing the risks of bureaucratic and authoritarian abuses present in a party that was so organized. The preceding assertion, according to which every action is either useful
or harmful only to the extent that it increases or hinders the party's
power, is tempered by no less important considerations. For example, Gramsci despised any party haughtiness: "Whoever replaces
important events with conceit, or carries out conceited politics, is
certainly to be suspected of a lack of seriousness" (Q, p. 1735).
Furthermore, he argues that, in order to achieve immediate political ends, one can protect one's privacy, but one must never fail to
tell the truth, since "in mass politics, to say the truth is precisely a
political necessity" (Q, p. 700).

End-of-Century Gramsci

1. After 1989

The International Gramscian Bibliography, compiled by the American historian John Cammett, includes more than ten thousand titles in many different languages, from Afrikaans, Albanian, Arabic, and Bengali, to Korean, Macedonian, Norwegian, Swedish and Turkish. The sheer magnitude of the collection might lead one to doubt whether it is still possible to say something new on Antonio Gramsci's life and work. And yet such doubt lasts briefly and a reaction arrives spontaneously. As we reach the end of his century, something new *must* be said about Gramsci. This is not so much to satisfy the need for originality at any cost, nor because of major changes in historiographic interpretation or of important recent discoveries of hitherto unknown writings. It is instead very likely that the last substantive innovation in Gramscian studies will remain the publication of the critical 1975 edition of *The Prison Notebooks*, which effectively opened the way to unforeseen methods of theoretical research and investigation. It is also true that with time some events that were difficult to interpret have been clarified as more comprehensive and reliable philological texts have been made available. There are other reasons that can bring forth a different perspective on Gramsci, besides the reconstruction of his life and work.

There are two events in particular that profoundly influenced the context within which Gramsci's contribution to national political events and contemporary Marxist thought were traditionally evaluated: the crisis of historical communism and the disappearance of the Italian Communist Party from the political scene.

"Communism is the near future of man's history, and the world will find its unification in it, not through an authoritarian, monopolistic one, but through spontaneity, with nations organically joining" ("*Vita politica internazionale* [II]" [International Political Life], ON, p. 20). Several decades have elapsed since Gramsci's ideas of the future. The anti-authoritarian movement of Chinese students is suppressed in blood in Tiananmen Square. We are horrified before the massacres by Nicolae Ceauşescu's Securitate in Timişoara and other Romanian cities. For the first time, Poland elects a non-Communist prime minister, Tadeusz Mazowiecki. The liberal-democratic Vaclav Havel is president of Czechoslovakia. After twenty-eight years, a breach is opened in the Berlin Wall—an event taken as a symbol of an epochal change. And, if that were not enough, two years later, the Soviet Union—the greatest power and beacon of communism worldwide since the Revolution of 1917—collapses into a confused Confederation of Independent States, irrevocably revealing its own political, economic, and social failure.

Before being an intellectual, scholar, and writer, Gramsci was a man of the party. "The party question . . . is central to Antonio Gramsci's entire activity, life, and thought." These are the words of Palmiro Togliatti, Gramsci's most authoritative comrade and collaborator. Returning to 1989, the secretary of the PCI announced another "turning point," which, with the 19th Extraordinary Congress, became the prelude to the foundation in 1991[1] of a post-Communist political formation, the present-day Democratic Party of the Left [*Partito Democratico della Sinistra*].[2]

2. Today and Tomorrow

In this context, the Gramscian experience appears to have definitely ended along with an entire historical phase, and, moreover, in total failure. In fact, it is difficult to imagine such a defeat as momentary for a movement that is supposed to be capable of shortly facing the forthcoming challenges and struggles for a worldwide "unification" of communism. On the other hand, it was not the occupying troops of a reactionary army who lowered the red flags of the Kremlin's towers, but the same people who raised them. Nor have extraordinary international laws, similar to those proclaimed by the fascist regime, intervened to dissolve the Italian Communist Party. It was rather the autonomous decision of the majority of its leaders and members. Nor has there been any resumption of the suppression of left intellectuals to the extent that it happened with American McCarthyism. Many of them started repudiating Marx and Lenin's ideas on their own account or for sheer opportunism.

Time has passed since the new postwar Italy, just awakening to freedom and democracy, saluted Gramsci's sacrifice in Mussolini's prisons and admired the literary and scientific work of the same mind that Il Duce tried to prevent from functioning for twenty years. It is a sort of hoax against despotic power. Indeed, it is still natural to remember Gramsci's moral and human teachings in view of current debates spurred by extreme historical revisionist trends in the study of European fascism and of the risk of seeing the lustrous pages of the nation's struggles for democracy expunged from public memory. It is quite another issue, however, to test the vitality of his political thought once it is severed from the communist perspective that guided it.

At first sight, the way to approach Gramsci seems to be taken for granted. It is enough to read his life's works knowing that these documents belong to another period worthy, despite everything, of being known and studied. It is a fascinating journey in contemporary cultural history to follow the intense life of one of the protagonists of the history of the national and international workers' movement, from the crisis of the Great War to the foundation of the Italian Communist Party and the coming of fascism; to grasp the lineaments of an original attempt to amend and critically develop Marx's theories in a constant comparison with those of other great thinkers; and to understand the impact of Gramsci's ideas on the ideological and political discussions of the second half of the twentieth century. But can Gramsci prove himself a suitable travelling companion for those who wish to understand the present and possibly foresee the future? This is probably so, but with some qualifications.

3. Why Two Gramscis?

It was 1937, the year of Gramsci's death, when Togliatti commemorated him as the crucial "party man." And rightly so, because Gramsci devoted his best days to the constitution, and later to the renewal and organization of the PCI. He was the party's general secretary and parliamentary representative. For being the party leader he received a prison sentence that eventually led to his death. In the final piece memorializing his old comrade, *Gramsci, un uomo* [Gramsci, A Man] (1964), Togliatti would ask himself whether Antonio Gramsci deserved to be placed "in a brighter light that transcends our party's historical vicissitudes."

It was no simple change of mind. During the 1960s it was becoming clear that a "second" Gramsci was drawing more attention than his activities as journalist and militant socialist, political leader, and antifascist. Since 1947, the year of the first publication of his *Letters from Prison*, and later, with the progressive publication in separate volumes of the *Prison Notebooks*, Italy and the world came in contact with a work of definitely universal value; it was destined, in short, to outlive the author's short existence. As proof of this, suffice it for now to consider the immense international bibliographies, the posthumous interest in these texts all over the world, the political, historical, philosophical, literary, and the anthropological research inspired by, or intertwined with, typically Gramscian concepts: hegemony, philosophy of praxis, national-popular, intellectual and moral reform, passive revolution, war of position, historic bloc, and so on.

Identifying two Gramscis does not imply contrasting the man of action with the thinker, nor does it imply any hypothesis about a radical change of opinion or political affiliation on his part. His ideas and theories find a common thread in the struggle for the emancipation of the subordinate classes as the cardinal point of an exemplary life. But the consequences of his arrest cut Gramsci's experience *de facto* into two parts. His participation in Italian public life and in the international communist movement, a decade long, is interrupted by the fascist court's prison sentence. This break is reflected in Gramsci's turn to solitary reflection (the *Prison Notebooks*) and to the writing of a torment-ridden diary (*Letters from Prison*). If, therefore, the first Gramsci indeed belonged to a well-defined and in many respects bygone era, "the Gramsci that matters most . . . is a posthumous author, whose work has become part of Italian and international culture in times different from those during which he lived, whose work could only be published when the period during which it was written—the time of fascism triumphant— had ended."[3] In short, it has become a classic of contemporary political thought, and, in light of his *Letters*, of twentieth-century Italian literature. And it is common to regard as a genuine classic that which resists context-contingency and continues to be the basis of dialogue in subsequent generations, despite being an expression of another time.

4. Politics and Truth

It can be said that Togliatti's initial attribution of Gramsci as "party man" over "intellectual" and "writer" should nowadays be reversed. As a matter of fact, this is already the prevailing position taken by critics in Italy and internationally. On the contrary, the occasional tendency of downplaying Gramsci's "legal" activity and political writings has resulted in diminishing their importance beyond measure or even making them invisible, along with their continuity with his later work. But beyond instances where there is a clear distortion of Gramsci's thought, considered politically "innocent,"[4] we must admit that the salient events are by now accurately dated and consigned to historical reconstruction and criticism, like his participation in the Turin Factory Councils movement, the managing of *Ordine Nuovo*, or his intervention in party debates preceding the Lyon Congress. His sharp commentaries on enduring and general themes like the political question of the role of intellectuals, the connections between philosophy, folklore, and common sense, or between the state and civil society remain relevant. Yet the problem is of a delicate nature, and presenting Gramsci primarily as a great intellectual requires caution simply because the relationship between intellectuals and politics is usually very complex.

For Julien Benda, a French author frequently discussed in Gramsci's *Notebooks*, intellectuals (the so-called "clerics"), who put their own scientific, artistic, and philosophic activity at the service of practical and political interests, strayed from their roles as custodians of justice and naked truth.[5] And this topic, which engaged Gramsci as well, is reappearing in contemporary debate.

According to Michel Foucault, "the political problem of intellectuals needs to be tackled not in terms of 'science/ideology,' but in terms of 'truth/power.' " The real political issue, in contrast, "is not mistake, illusion, alienated conscience, or ideology, but rather truth itself."[6] Edward Said maintains that the primary task of the intellectual is "speaking truth to power."[7] Even Sartre, the famous supporter of "engagement" by cultured men, held that "the exploited classes do not need an *ideology*, but a practical truth about society."[8]

Hannah Arendt, political philosopher, well summarized what she defines as "a common place":

No one has ever questioned the fact that truth and politics have a bad relationship with each other, and no one that I know has ever listed sincerity among political virtues. Lies have always been considered necessary and legitimate instruments not only by the professional politician or demagogue, but also by the statesman. Why is it so? And what does it mean, on the one hand, for the nature and dignity of a political environment, and, on the other, for the nature and dignity of truth and sincerity? Is it perhaps characteristic of the very same essence of truth to be impotent, and characteristic of the very same essence of power to be deceptive?[9]

Gramsci would have agreed with respect to "a common place." In fact, he wrote in the *Notebooks*:

There is a widespread opinion in many circles (a sign of the political and cultural level of these circles) that lying is essential to the art of politics, to be able to shrewdly hide one's own true opinions and the real purposes to which one tends, to be able to make one believe the opposite of what one really wants, etc. This is so rooted and widespread an opinion that when the truth is actually said, no one believes it. (Q, p. 699)

Nonetheless, Gramsci would not have shared the notion of truth as a prerogative of disinterested culture and science and politics as necessarily based on deceit. In fact, in his view, "in politics, one could speak of discretion, not of falsehood in the narrow-minded sense thought of by many: in mass politics, to tell the truth is precisely a political necessity" (Q, pp. 699–700).

5. Truth and Hegemony

It is useful to keep in mind that the concept of truth is not univocal. To draw from a simple but commonly accepted distinction that Hannah Arendt made her own, there are in fact "rational truths" and "factual truths." In the former are included mathematical, scientific, and philosophical truths, i.e., general and abstract principles, the specific unit of epistemological analyses and procedures. In contrast, it is facts and events that dominate the field of politics. Therefore, it is at the more modest factual truths that one needs to look, like the "role, during the Russian Revolution, of a man named Trotsky, whose name does not appear in any book on the history of Soviet Russia." This example is a case in point because it shows both that factual truths "are more vulnerable than all types of rational truths combined" (it is easier to slander an opponent than denying that two by two equals four), and that, indeed, "there are very few chances for factual truths to survive the assault of power."[10]

However, even as an intellectual, Gramsci was not only uninterested in hypothetical rational truths, but he did not even intend to defend factual truths as concealed or distorted by political power. This traditional task of the intellectual did not belong to him. "Telling the truth" was to him not the first and foremost moral imperative of an honest man of culture. It was a "political necessity" closely tied to the main concept of his theoretical perspective, hegemony.

As militant communist, Gramsci was against the hegemony of bourgeois and authoritarian regimes, which exercised power over the proletariat. As a Marxist thinker, he tried to elaborate an alternative hegemonic theory that would enable the exploited classes to independently lead the entire social apparatus and system of economic production. To fight a political opponent, it is first necessary to know and understand the mechanisms through which power succeeds in imposing itself. In the case of overtly authoritarian regimes, the problem related to truth becomes secondary. In fact, by definition, dictators and oligarchies do not care about earning the consent of the subordinate classes. In general, they neither lie nor bother to conceal their interests and purposes. They can even genuinely flaunt their abuse of power and tyrannical intentions for propaganda purposes—and as a warning to the opposition—since they govern through violent coercion. Bourgeois-democratic power, instead, tends to disguise the real nature of their social and economic interests. They conceal the truth for the purpose of gaining passive consent, passed off as free agreement or even active support. The type of consent asked of revolutionary masses, the future subjects of self-government, is of a different nature. These are the "organisms" for which Gramsci considered of "vital importance an active and direct consent and not a passive and indirect one" (Q, p. 1771). To achieve this, it is essential to use the *method* of "telling the truth," which, nevertheless, is neither an "act of enlightenment from the top" (perhaps by an uncorrupted intellectual elite) nor "something that appears suddenly or is acquired peacefully."[11]

6. Reform of Politics

But is it truly possible to resolve the historic incompatibility between truth and politics? Gramsci noted that "there never was a moral and intellectual reform in Italy that involved the popular masses." This phenomenon is not comparable to the sixteenth-century Protestant Reformation and its influence on the "public spirit." In addition, "the Renaissance, eighteenth-century French philosophy, and nineteenth-century German philosophy were reforms that only touched the higher classes and often only intellectuals" (Q, p. 515). Gramsci consequently thought that a function of true renewal and progress, such as to cover "all society down to its deepest roots," could be had through "historical materialism," Marx's theory based on the critique of economics and the treatment of all socioeconomic formations as transitory. Even "cultural reform," that is, the "civil uplifting of the depressed strata of society," is affected by the economic structure. "Therefore, a moral and intellectual reform cannot but be connected to a program of economic reform. This is precisely the concrete way of presenting a program for moral and intellectual reform" (Q, p. 1561).

The problem extends to the most fundamental political element, the party, which, in turn, "must and cannot be but the announcer and organizer of a moral and intellectual reform. In sum, this means preparing the ground for further developing a national popular collective will toward the fulfilment of a higher and complete reform of modern civilization" (Q, p. 1560).

"Intellectual and moral," these are the adjectives that indicate the sense of Gramsci's hypothesis on cultural, political, and economic reform. Thus the method of truth returns as the objective of intellectual research and the foundation of every conception of morals. In any case, in tracing the history of modern socialism and its mistakes, it is easy to see that no attempt was ever made to carry out a holistic reform close to Gramsci's understandings. Something went missing as time passed. And so, wherever in the East changes in the relations of production took place, the parties in power made chaff out of truth and deprived intellectuals of the right to express it. In Western liberal democracies, the truth offered by opposition intellectuals created nothing but small cur-

rents of opinion, so inadequate with respect to promoting substantive economic system reforms that, in the end, they gave up
any such attempts for good. Even the PCI, at least formally the
most Gramscian in the world, did not escape accusations of prac-
ticing a "double truth." This happened to such an extent that perhaps one should reflect on the reason why Togliatti, polemically
considered a champion of Communist "duplicity," concluded his
Gramsci, un uomo, written a couple of months before his death,
by remembering "the ruthless truth" that marked Gramsci's work
"in his struggle not only to understand the world but also to
transform it."

7. Transitory Victories and Apparent Defeats

What has been put forward thus far is only one of the possible
readings that can contribute to determining whether and to what
extent Gramsci has been left unscathed by the failure of historic
Communist experience. Certainly, one could offer others, perhaps more complex and sophisticated readings. Nevertheless,
Gramsci's recovery of truth in politics remains indeed a very
timely theme. In any event, even the last serious attempt at
reforming really existing socialism before its collapse, Mikhail
Gorbachev's *perestroika*, was linked to *glasnost*, that is, to trans-
parency in every sector of public life. "What is important is the
truth,"[12] the Soviet president declared. It is not even necessary to
mention the powerful laboratories of political manipulation
implanted in the West in the last few years (with Italy in the front
line), based on controlling the means of information and mass
media. We can rather state that now, more than ever, the latter has
become a decisive factor in exercising hegemony and seizing consent. To this must be added the widespread revulsion caused by
numerous political scandals, cases of corruption and racial intol-
erance, and the criminal contamination of personalities in power.

Furthermore, virtualized procedures are grafted[13] onto phenomena such as wars and the globalization of financial markets, which obscure and make the very concrete realities of millions of human beings almost incomprehensible. It is therefore natural that at the end of the millennium the political sphere looks like a foreign and hostile entity that breeds disillusionment and passivity. In spite of it all, no solution is given to current problems, nor are there prospects for the future outside political games and relations of political power.

Antonio Gramsci was often described as a defeated man, a "loser" in modern parlance. Considering his tormented life and the current fate of the movement to which he devoted his hard intellectual work, perhaps this is not incorrect. However, it is necessary to abandon the framework of a cynical concept of politics, according to which might makes right. It is not difficult to show how shortsighted this conception is. In fact, can one consider the winners of the past to be the winners of today? Did they really win?

Think of Mussolini, who used his despotic power to beat and extinguish one of the most insightful minds opposing the regime. Or consider the Russian Stalinist leadership, to whom a barely known "Sardinian hunchback" dared to level a grave accusation about the bureaucratic and authoritarian slope on which the Bolshevik Party was beginning to slip. In subsequent times, Italy, a wounded country, would condemn fascist crimes without appeal, and would turn to the pages of *Letters from Prison* as a testament to a personal tragedy ready to go around the world. In the streets of Moscow and Leningrad crowds were knocking down the statues of the protagonists and symbols of a communism existing only on paper; on five continents, intellectuals and militants who sided with exploited workers and oppressed peoples were undertaking the study of the *Notebooks* to look for innovative ways toward civil progress, peace, and democratic coexistence.

These are the horizons of what Gramsci defined as "major politics," as opposed to "minor politics (day-to-day politics, parliamentary politics, politics of lobbying and intrigue)."

> High politics deals with questions related to the foundation of new states, and the struggle for the destruction, defense, and conservation of given organic socioeconomic structures. Minor politics is related to the partial and daily issues taken up within an already established structure for the struggle for primacy among different factions of the same political class. (Q, pp. 1563–64)

One needs only to read a newspaper to see how most of today's national and international political processes and arrangements are of modest dimensions, both practically and ideally. In effect, Gramsci has little to say about politics of limited scope, to which many have turned their back. If Gramsci is not relevant in these cases, it is because "major politics," which goes beyond the simple administrative tasks and does not evade issues and changes of extraordinary scope, has lost topicality as well. Justice, freedom, equality—even the fundamental right to life, in fact, are not mere components of moral philosophy, but ends specific to political democracy that have not yet been achieved everywhere. If they continue to stand on the sidelines, then indeed Gramsci's ideas will definitely be defeated. However, a defeat of Gramsci's ideas could also signify a collective defeat. Certainly, the articles in *Avanti!* and *Ordine Nuovo*, as well as in the *Notebooks* and the *Letters*, require a selective reading—based on separating dated material and uncertain and provisional results from conceptual tools—if they are to remain valid in confronting current problems.

Biographical Chronology
of Antonio Gramsci

1891 Born in Ales, near Cagliari, January 22.

1911 Graduated from Lyceum in Cagliari; in November he enrolls at the Department of Literature, University of Turin.

1913 Joins the socialist section of Turin.

1915 On December 10, joins the Turin editorial staff of *Avanti!*

1917 Continues his journalistic activity and becomes director of *Grido del Popolo* [The People's Cry]. Elected secretary of the temporary executive committee of the socialist section of Turin.

1918 *Grido del Popolo* ceases publication.

1919   With Tasca, Terracini, and Togliatti, he founds *Ordine
        Nuovo* [New Order]. The first issue appears on May 1st.

1920   In September, he takes part in the factory occupation
        movement. On December 24, the last issue of the
        weekly *Ordine Nuovo* is printed.

1921   On January 1st, the first issue of the daily *Ordine
        Nuovo*, organ of the Turin Communists, appears. On
        January 21, he is elected member of the executive com-
        mittee of the Italian Communist Party, formed the same
        day in Livorno.

1922   In March, he is elected to represent the party in the
        executive committee of the Communist International.
        On March 26, he leaves for Moscow. In June, he partici-
        pates in the Second Congress of the International. He
        is admitted to a clinic in Moscow, where, in September,
        he meets his future wife, Julia Schucht.

1923   During his stay in Moscow, the Italian police issue a
        warrant for his arrest. On December 3, he arrives in
        Vienna, elected by the International's executive, and
        tasked with maintaining contacts between the Italian
        Communist Party and other European Communist
        parties.

1924   On February 22, the first issue of *l'Unità* [Unity] is
        printed in Milan. The third series of *Ordine Nuovo*, now
        a fortnightly publication, is printed in Rome beginning
        March 1. On April 6th, he is elected deputy in the
        Veneto constituency. He returns to Italy on May 12. In
        August, his son Delio is born in Moscow.

1925   In January, he meets Tatiana Schucht, Julia's sister, in
        Rome. He takes part in the 5th Session of the
        International Executive in Moscow in March and April.

1926   In January, he participates in the 3rd National Congress
        of the PCI in Lyon. Julia gives birth in August to a sec-
        ond son, Giuliano, in Moscow. On November 8, despite
        parliamentary immunity, he is arrested and imprisoned
        in Regina Coeli. On November 18, he receives a five-
        year sentence of solitary confinement. On December 7,
        he arrives on the island of Ustica.

1927   On January 14, the military court of Milan issues a war-
        rant for his arrest. He leaves Ustica on January 20, and
        on February 7 he is sent to San Vittore prison.

1928   On March 19, he is tried by the Special Court. On
        May 11, he leaves for Rome and the following day is
        imprisoned at Regina Coeli. On May 28, the trial
        against the leadership of the PCI starts. On June 4,
        he is sentenced to twenty years, four months, and five
        days in prison. On June 22, he is assigned to the
        special prison in Turi, near Bari, where he arrives on
        July 19.

1929   On February 8, he begins to write the first of his *Prison
        Notebooks*.

1931   Already severely ill, in August he is affected by a serious
        health crisis.

1932   Following amnesty measures, his sentence is reduced to
        twelve years and four months.

1933   On March 7, he is struck by a second serious health cri-
        sis. In July, he asks Tatiana to initiate a petition for his
        transfer to the infirmary of another prison. The petition
        is accepted in October and, on November 19, he leaves
        Turi and is temporarily assigned to Civitavecchia. On
        December 7, still under arrest, he is admitted to Doctor
        Cusumano's clinic in Formia.

1934   He forwards a request for conditional freedom, which
        is granted on October 25.

1935   In April, he asks to be transferred to a private clinic in
        Fiesole (near Florence). In June, he suffers a third
        health crisis. On August 24, he leaves Cusumano's
        clinic and is admitted to the Quisisana clinic in Rome.

1937   With the end of conditional freedom in April, his full
        freedom is restored. On April 25, he suffers a cerebral
        hemorrhage. He dies on April 27. The funeral takes
        place the day after. His ashes are buried at the Verano
        Cemetery in Rome and, following liberation, trans-
        ferred to the Protestent Cemetery.

Biographies of Main Political Figures

BARBOUSSE, HENRY (1873–1935). French novelist and journalist. During World War I he took an active part in antimilitarism and pacifism through his actions and writings. A Communist, he published *Clarity* in 1919, and *Lenin* and *Stalin* in the 1930s. He lived for many years in the Soviet Union and died in Moscow.

BARTOLI, MATTEO GIULIO (1873–1946). Linguist and Professor of Linguistics at the University of Turin, where he was Gramsci's teacher. Founder of "Spatial Linguistics," a method that derived the chronology of linguistic events through observation of their geographical distribution. His works include: *Introduzione alla neolinguistica* [Introduction to Neo-linguistics] (1925) and *Saggi di linguistica spaziale* [Essay on Spatial Linguistics] (1945).

BORDIGA, AMADEO (1889–1970). Became a member of the Socialist Party when a student of engineering in Naples. After the end of World War I, he founded the weekly *Il Soviet* [The

Soviet]. Printed from December 1918 to April 1922, in 1919 it became the organ of the Communist Abstentionist faction of PSI. After the Livorno scission, he was secretary of PCI until 1923. He was arrested in 1923 and spent from 1927 to 1930 in solitary confinement. In 1930 he was accused by the Comintern of Trotskyism and expelled from the party. After his expulsion, he left militant politics.

BUKHARIN, NIKOLAI IVANOVIC (1888–1938). Bolshevik since 1906, forced into exile in Scandinavia and in the United States, he went back to Russia in 1917 and played an important role in the October Revolution. Author of theoretical works, in 1918 he became part of the Left Communists. However, during the 1920s he was the strongest supporter of NEP (New Economic Policy). He was Stalin's ally in the fight against the left opposition, but in 1929 he was excluded from any position and accused of "right-wing drift." Arrested in 1937, he was tried and executed in 1938.

COSMO, UMBERTO (1868–1944). Taught literature in various lyceums in Italy, in Turin, from 1898. An antifascist, he was forced to leave academia in 1926. As a literary critic, he contributed in particular to Dante studies with works like *La vita di Dante* [The Life of Dante] in 1930 and *L'ultima ascesa* [The Last Ascent] in 1936.

CROCE, BENEDETTO (1866–1952). A philosopher, he exercised great influence on twentieth-century Italian culture. A pupil of Antonio Labriola and a Marxist scholar, he nevertheless gained greater affinity for idealism, seeing all reality as history (absolute historicism) and a product of the human spirit. At the beginning of the century, he took on a central position as aesthetic innovator. In politics, he was a great supporter of liberalism. Elected senator in 1910, he became minister of public education in 1920–1921, and minister without portfolio in 1943-1944. A Hegelian, he integrated Hegel's "dialectic of the opposites" with the so-called "dialectic of the separate," according to which the spirit is divided into four categories, two of them related to theoretical activity (aesthetic and logic) and the other two being part of practice (economic and ethic). His works include: *Estetica come scienza dell'espressione e linguistica generale* [Aesthetics as General Science of Expression and Linguistics] (1908); *Logica come scienza del concetto puro* [Logic as Science of Pure Concept] (1908); *Filosofia della pratica. Economia ed etica* [Philosophy of Practice: Economics and Ethics] (1909); *Teoria e storia della storiografia* [Theory and History of Historiography] (1917); *Materialismo storico e economia marxistica* [Historical Materialism and Marxist Economics] (1918); *La storia come pensiero e azione* [History as Thought and Action] (1938).

DE AMICIS, EDMONDO (1846-1908). Journalist and scholar, wrote his most popular works, *Gli amici* [Friends] (1883) and more importantly *Cuore* [Heart] (1886), when he shifted his interest from the bourgeois world to that of the working classes. A typical exponent of a certain nineteenth-century pedagogic and paternalistic literature, he denounced the miserable conditions of the Italian emigrants with *Sull' oceano* [On the Ocean] (1889) and tackled the issue related to popular schools with *Il romanzo di un maestro* [A Teacher's Novel] (1890).

DE SANCTIS, FRANCESCO (1817-1883). Literary critic, and a liberal, he elaborated his method and critical theory under the influence of Hegel's *Aesthetic*. He took part in the Neapolitan insurrection of 1848. He was arrested, and after three years in prison he was sent into exile. He first taught in Turin and later at the Polytechnic University of Zurich. After the unification of Italy, he was elected parliamentary deputy and minister of public instruction. Among his works, in which he theorized about the autonomy of art and the inseparable nexus between content and form, are *Saggi critici* [Critical Essays] (1866) and *Storia della letteratura italiana* [History of Italian Literature] (1870–1871). The story of his political experience is told in his autobiographical writing *Un viaggio elettorale* [An Electoral Voyage] (1875).

ENGELS, FRIEDRICH (1820–1895). Founder, together with Karl Marx, of scientific socialism. Hegelian at first, he very soon approached communism. In 1848, together with Marx, he published *Manifesto of the Communist Party*. In the same year, he took part in revolutionary insurrections and in the following years he became involved in the organization of the proletarian movement. In 1870, he settled in London and, after Marx's death in 1883, became the natural leader of the international workers' movement and took care of the coordination of the various centers of social-democratic political action, following the foundation of the Second International (1889). He dedicated himself to intensive study of the theoretical problems of communism. His works include: *The Situation of the Working Class in England* (1845), *Anti-Dühring* (1878), and the posthumous *Dialectics of Nature* (1883).

FEUERBACH, LUDWIG (1804–1872). German philosopher. A Hegelian in his youth, he later became one of Hegel's harshest critics, reproaching him for having dissolved reality into pure abstract logic. Hence, his attempt to reverse Hegelian dialectics by immersing it in the pragmatism of needs and human feelings. Philosophy must, therefore, become *anthropology*, that is, man must be its supreme object, as *real being* or *sensitive*. His works include: *The Essence of Christianity* (1841), *Principles of the Philosophy of the Future* (1844), and *The Essence of Religion* (1845).

FORTUNATO, GIUSTINO (1848–1932). Politician and writer, he was mostly devoted to the study of the Southern Question, making the country aware of the social and political problems connected to the backwardness of the South. Member of the right, from 1880 to 1909, during this last year he was elected senator. His works include: *La questione demaniale nelle province meridionali* [The State Question in the Southern Provinces] (1882), *Il Mezzogiorno e lo Stato italiano* [Southern Italy and the Italian State] (1911), and *Questione meridionale e riforma tributaria* [The Southern Question and the Tax Reform] (1920).

GENTILE, GIOVANNI (1875–1944). Idealist philosopher, he proposed to reform Hegel's dialectical philosophy, claiming that only the process of thinking (actualism) is a dialectical process, or development. At first a collaborator in Benedetto Croce's *Critica*, but later broke with him. In 1923 he joined fascism. Minister of public instruction, from 1922 to 1924, he started a comprehensive reform of the school system. His works include: *La riforma della dialettica hegeliana* [The Reform of Hegelian Dialectic] (1913), *Teoria generale dello spirito come atto puro* [General Theory of the Spirit as Pure Act] (1916), and *Sistema di logica come teoria del conoscere* [System of Logic as Theory of Knowledge] (1917–1922).

GIOLITTI, GIOVANNI (1842–1928). Politician, liberal deputy since 1882, he was elected minister many times and became president of the council. He promoted industrial economic development, tolerating a peaceful growth of the workers and socialists' movement. An anti-interventionist, he returned to the political scene in 1919. As president of the Council in 1920–1921 he underestimated the rising fascist movement, convinced it would be able to be absorbed within the form of the liberal state. Only after the Matteotti crime (1924) did he turn to open opposition.

GOBETTI, PIERO (1901–1926). Freelance journalist, he founded, in 1918, the biweekly review *Energie nuove* [New Energies], which, like Gaetano Salvemini's *l'Unità*, tried to suggest concrete solutions to the political problems of the early postwar period. The review ceased its publication in 1920. Following suggestions from *Ordine Nuovo* and the Factory Councils Movement, *Energie nuove* was developing a radical liberalism that saw in the Turin working class the model of a new leading elite. These themes were more specifically formulated in the review *La rivoluzione liberale* [Liberal Revolution], founded in 1922, whose purpose was to contribute to the formation of a political class aware of the need for the working classes to participate in the life of the state. In 1924, he founded *Il Baretti*. Because of his fighting against fascist dictatorship, on September 5, 1924, he was assaulted by a fascist squad. Forced to suspend the publication of *Rivoluzione liberale*, he moved to Paris to escape increasing persecution, where he died shortly afterward. His works include: *La rivoluzione liberale* [The Liberal Revolution] (1922), *Risorgimento senza eroi* [Risorgimento without Heroes] (1926), and *Paradosso dello spirito russo* [The Paradox of the Russian Spirit] (1926).

GRIECO, RUGGERO (1893–1955). He joined socialism at a very young age. In the Socialist Party's internal struggles he sided with the revolutionary left and, in 1919, he joined the abstentionist fraction. After the Livorno scission, he was elected to the central committee and the executive of the PCI. Arrested in 1923 and acquitted for lack of evidence, after his release he was entrusted the organization of the party's agrarian section. Elected deputy in 1924, he sided with Gramsci at the Lyon Congress. In 1929, he represented the Italian party at the Communist International in Moscow. In charge of the agrarian section of PCI, he became a member of the leadership. Elected to the Constituent, he became senator in 1948.

HEGEL, GEORG WILHELM FRIEDRICH (1770–1831). Philosopher, major exponent of the so-called "objective idealism" of nineteenth-century German philosophy. In his system, the world of nature, history, and spiritual production was exposed for the first time as a process that functions according to objective laws, that is, independent of ideas, aspirations, and the will of single individuals. He conceived it like a constant movement, change, and development of which he attempted to demonstrate internal connections. Among his most important works are: *Phenomenology of Spirit* (1807), *Science of Logic* (1812-1816), and *Elements of the Philosophy of Right* (1821).

IBSEN, HENRIK (1828-1906). Norwegian playwright, he exercised great influence on European theater and culture. Already author of important works like *Peer Gynt* (1867), since 1875 he showed an interest in the bourgeois world, whose conventions he subjected to careful and harsh examination in a series of plays, including: *A Doll's House* (1879), *Ghosts* (1881), and *An Enemy of the People* (1882).

KAMENEV [pseudonym of Lev Borisovic Rosenfeld] (1883-1936). Russian politician, from 1901 he adhered to the left wing of the Social Democratic Party. Bolshevik by 1903, he was deported to Siberia in 1914. Freed after the February Revolution, he influenced Bolshevik politics until Lenin's return. Member of the Political Office and president of the "Soviet" in Moscow, he formed the so-called "*troika*" in 1922, with Stalin and Zinoviev. After 1925, he was part of the left opposition, and in 1927 was removed from his positions. Reinstated after self-criticism, he was arrested again in 1935, then tried and executed in 1936.

LABRIOLA, ANTONIO (1843-1904). Philosopher, pupil of Bertrando Spaventa in Naples, he studied Hegel and Spinoza. Later, he was influenced by Herbart. In 1874, he obtained the chair of moral philosophy at the University of Rome. He adhered to socialism, but was always in a difficult relationship with the

PSI. He worked to disseminate historical materialism and supported a critical Marxism contrasting with revisionist trends that emerged in the International after Engels's death. Among his works, of particular importance are his essays *In memoria del Manifesto dei comunisti* [In Memory of the Communist Manifesto] (1896), *Del materialismo storico* [Of Historical Materialism] (1897), and *Discorrendo di socialismo e di filosofia* [Discourse on Socialism and Philosophy] (1898), the latter in letter format and addressed to Sorel.

LENIN, V.I. [pseudonym of Vladimir Illyich Ulyanov] (1870–1924). Main architect of the Russian Revolution. Beginning in 1893 he distributed Marxist propaganda among workers in Saint Petersburg. Arrested, he was deported to Siberia in 1897 and later emigrated abroad. He returned to his homeland when the revolution broke out in 1905 and carried on intense political activity. Again forced to emigrate, he remained abroad until the 1917 March Revolution. That year, he came back and assumed the leadership of the revolutionary insurrection. After the October Revolution, he became head of the Soviet government. Together with his political activity, he was also active as a theoretician of Communism with works like *What Is To be Done?* (1902), *Materialism and Empirio-Criticism* (1909), and *The State and Revolution* (1917).

LORIA, ACHILLE (1857–1943). Economist and sociologist of the school of positivism, university teacher. Author of various writings inspired by historical materialism, but not Marx; especially concerned with the theory of value. Among his works: *La legge di popolazione e il sistema sociale* [The Law of Population and the Social System] (1882), *Analisi della proprieta' capitalistica* [Analysis of Capitalist Property] (1889), *La sintesi economica* [Economic Synthesis] (1909), and *La dinamica economica* [Economic Dynamics] (1935).

LUNACHARSKY, ANATOLY VASILYEVICH (1875-1933). Russian politician, Marxist historian of art and literature. A militant revolutionary since 1892, he participated in the organization of the Bolshevik faction, from which he later separated to form an autonomous Menshevik group. His work *Religion and Socialism* (1908) was harshly criticized by Lenin because it was an attempt to reconcile religious issues and socialism. Again Bolshevik, he was people's commissar of education after the 1917 Revolution, until 1929.

MARX, KARL (1818-1883). Economist and philosopher, founder of scientific socialism. As a youth, he belonged to the so-called "Left-Hegelian" current. In 1848, he stated the principles of his theory in *Manifesto of the Communist Party*, written in collaboration with Friedrich Engels. In 1849, he settled in London where he founded the International Workingmen's Association (the First International). In 1867, the first volume of his fundamental work, *Capital*, appeared. The second and third volumes were published posthumously, with Engels as editor, in 1885 and 1894, respectively. His works include: *The Poverty of Philosophy* (1847), *A Contribution to the Critique of Political Economy* (1859), *Theories of Surplus Value* (1862), and *Critique of the Gotha Program* (1875).

MATTEOTTI, GIACOMO (1885-1924). Close to socialism since his young years, he soon became involved in political and unionist activities. Elected parliamentary deputy in 1919 and 1921. As reformist and Turati's friend, he joined the United Socialist Party, becoming its secretary in 1922. An uncompromising anti-fascist, he was reelected deputy in 1924, although he denounced the atmosphere of illegality surrounding the electoral campaign and the elections. Abducted by a fascist squad on June 10, 1924, his body was found near Rome on August 16, 1924.

MUSSOLINI, BENITO (1883–1945). Founder and *Duce* of fascism. At first a socialist, he was a member of the party's leadership and director of *Avanti!* At the beginning of World War I, he abandoned the neutral position of the PSI and became a strong interventionist. Expelled from the party, he founded the newspaper *Il Popolo d'Italia* [The People of Italy]. At the end of the war, he gave rise to the "Italian Combat Squad" in Milan. Elected parliamentary deputy in 1921, he organized fascist squads, theorizing the winning of power with violence. After the 1922 march on Rome, he was summoned by the king to form a cabinet, together with some other exponents of the Liberal and Popular parties. After Matteotti's murder in 1924, he achieved absolute power and established a totalitarian regime. He allied with Nazi Germany during World War II but as the German defeat took shape his personal power came to an end. Arrested by order of the king and later freed by the Germans in 1945, he was placed at the head of the Italian Social Republic, which included territories controlled by the Nazi occupation troops. During the partisan uprising in Northern Italy, he was captured and executed.

PASCOLI, GIOVANNI (1855–1912). A poet, he adhered to socialism during his university studies. Later, he devoted himself to teaching and poetry. Among his poems is *Myricae* (1891), whose dominant theme is the countryside. Pascoli considered that the poet's inspiration was something prodigiously instinctive, as expressed in the fundamental document of his poetry, *Il fanciullino* [The Little Child]. Other collections of poems include: *Canti di Castelvecchio* [Songs of Castelvecchio] (1903), *Odi e inni* [Odes and Hymns] (1906), and the posthumous *Poemi del Risorgimento* [Poems of the Risorgimento].

PIRANDELLO, LUIGI (1867–1936). Dramatist and novelist, he exercised great influence on twentieth-century literature. Awarded the Nobel Prize in 1934. The foundation of his work is the defeat

of a generation and the historical experience of the petit bourgeoisie, above all that of the South, disappointed by the new
authoritarian and bureaucratic Italian state. Critical of optimistic
idealism, vitalism, and Dannunzianism, his dialectic aims to stimulate a real interest in the human drama, a truth to nature that is
neither mystical nor rhetorical and beyond appearance. Among
his numerous dramatic works are *Cosi' e' (se vi pare)* [So It Is (If
You Think So)] (1917), *Enrico IV* [Henry IV] (1922), and *Questa
sera si recita a soggetto* [Tonight We Improvise] (1930).

PREZZOLINI, GIUSEPPE (1882–1982). Writer and journalist,
organizer of important cultural enterprises since the beginning of
the twentieth century. Co-founder with Giovanni Papini of *Il
Leonardo* [Leonard], he started the review *La Voce* [The Voice] in
1914. He lived in Paris and then in the United States until the end
of World War II. His sentimental nationalism led him to join fascism. His writings include: *La cultura Italiana* [Italian Culture]
(1923); *Vita di N. Machiavelli fiorentino* [The Life of the
Florentine N. Machiavelli] (1927); *America in pantofole* [America
in Slippers] (1950); *America con gli stivali* [America in Boots]
(1954); and his autobiography, *L'italiano inutile* [The Useless
Italian] (1954).

RICARDO, DAVID (1772–1823). English stockbroker and economist, main exponent of the *classical school*. Examined income
distribution among landowners, capitalists, and workers and its
influence on the development of an economic system, using the
labor theory of value. Author of the *Essay on the Influence of a
Low Price of Corn on the Profits of Stocks* (1815) and *On the
Principles of Political Economy and Taxation* (1821).

ROLLAND, ROMAIN (1866–1944). French writer. Former
musicologist and later successful novelist with the cycle *Jean-
Christophe*, ten volumes published between 1904 and 1912, in

which the author exposed his anti-conformist and progressive viewpoints through the life of an imaginary German musician. He also wrote long essays on famous historical and cultural personalities like Michelangelo, Gandhi, Goethe, and Tolstoy. Awarded the Nobel Prize in 1915, the same year he published a series of articles under the title *Above the Battle* in which he expressed his pacifist position. After the war, he gravitated toward Communism.

SALVEMINI, GAETANO (1873–1957). Historian and politician. Initially, he dedicated himself to the study of medieval history. University professor in Messina and Pisa, and from 1916 onward in Florence. Member of the PSI since the end of the nineteenth century, his activity was centered around the Southern Question and trying to direct the socialist movement toward pro-southern positions. Critical of the party, which he considered too favorable to Giolitti, he left the PSI in 1911 and founded the weekly *l'Unità* [Unity], in whose pages he committed himself to forming a secular and progressive public opinion. Elected parliamentary deputy in 1919, he was a firm opponent of Mussolini. Arrested in 1925, after his release in August of that year, he left Italy. He first lived in France, then England, and in 1934 settled in the United States. He returned to his country in 1947, where he resumed his university teaching in Florence and his contributions to various periodicals. His works include: *La Rivoluzione francese* [The French Revolution] (1906), *La dittatura fascista in Italia* [The Fascist Dictatorship in Italy] (1927), and *La politica estera italiana dal 1871 al 1914* [Italian Foreign Policy from 1871 to 1914] (1944).

SCOCCIMARRO, MAURO (1895–1972). He was one of the founders of the PCI in 1921. An anti-fascist, in 1926 he was arrested and sentenced to twenty years in prison. Freed in 1943, he took an active part to the Resistance and became Prime Minister of occupied Italy in Bonomi's second government

(1944), then Minister of Finances with Parri (1945), and De Gasperi's first two governments (1946–1947). He was senator from 1948.

SERRATI, GIACINTO MENOTTI (1872–1926). Socialist, participated in the congress for the foundation of the PSI. Arrested several times between 1895 and 1898, he emigrated to the United States, from where he directed the newspaper *Il Proletario* [The Proletarian] from 1902. He returned to Italy in 1911, and in October 1914 was offered the position of director of *Avanti!* An anti-interventionist, he was arrested and sentenced after the 1917 popular insurrection in Turin and released at the end of the war. Head of the maximalist-electionist faction of the PSI, in the review *Communism*, which he directed from 1919 to 1920, he supported a political line favorable to joining the Comintern and opposed to the expulsion of reformists. After joining the Third Internationalist faction in 1922, he joined the PCI in 1924.

SOREL, GEORGES (1847–1922). French writer and politician. His interests centered around the problems of technique and the philosophy of science, acquiring a relativistic conception of scientific truth. Later, he devoted himself to historical, economic, and political studies, and through his knowledge of Proudhon and Marx he passed from liberal conservatism to socialism. He was a regular contributor to the reviews *Ère Nouvelle* and *Devenir Social*. Critical of schematic and deterministic interpretations that prevailed within the international socialist movement at the time, he became the main theoretician of French and European revolutionary unionism. During his last years, he expressed prefernce toward the Bolshevik revolution and was an admirer of Lenin. His ideas of *myth* and *violence*, anti-parliamentarism, and revolutionary voluntarism influenced many intellectuals in the first decades of the twentieth century. His works include: *The Decomposition of Marxism* (1908) and *Reflections on Violence* (1908).

SRAFFA, PIERO (1898–1983). Economist, professor at Perugia and Cagliari, and from 1927, in Cambridge. He initiated the studies of imperfect competition with his writings *Sulle relazioni fra costo e quantità prodotta* [On the Relationship Between Cost and Produced Quantity] (1925) and *Le leggi della produttività in regime di concorrenza* [Laws of Productivity in a Regime of Competition] (1926). With *Produzione di merci a mezzo di merci* [Production of Commodities through Commodities] (1960), he examined price ranges in relation to distributional change, showing the inconsistency of some tenets of classical theory.

STALIN, JOSEF [pseudonym of Iosif Vissarionovich Dzhugashvili] (1879–1953). Member of the Russian Social Democratic Party since 1898, he became an active revolutionary at a very young age and was arrested several times by Tsarist police. Deported to Siberia for five years, he returned to Russia in 1917 after the Tsarist regime was overthrown. When the Bolsheviks won power, he assumed the position of People's Commissar. Elected General Secretary of the Communist Party in 1922, he further strengthened his power. After Lenin's death, a harsh conflict erupted between Stalin and Trotsky that ended with the latter's defeat and expulsion from the party. In 1928, he began a policy of agrarian industrialization and collectivization (five-year plans) that was the subject of harsh internal opposition, and was subdued by the purges and trials of 1934–1938. In 1941, he assumed the position of President of the Council, maintaining this office throughout World War II.

TASCA, ANGELO (1892–1960). Joined the socialist section of Turin in 1912 and took part in the founding of *Ordine Nuovo* [New Order] in 1921. Among the founders of the Communist Party, he was one of the most important exponents of the Right faction. Forced to go into exile during fascism, he became an officer of the Communist International. An anti-Stalinist, he was expelled from the Communist Party in 1929 and thereafter joined the PSI. His works include: *Nascita e avvento del fascismo* [The Birth and Coming of Fascism] (1949) and *I primi dieci anni del PCI* [The First Ten Years of the PCI] (1953).

TERRACINI, UMBERTO (1895-1983). Secretary of the Piedmontese Socialist Youth Federation in 1914 and the Turin Federation of the PSI in 1919, he was among the promoters of *Ordine Nuovo*. He took part in the founding of the PCI. Director of *l'Unità* in 1926, he was arrested in August of the same year and sentenced to twenty-three years' imprisonment by the Special Court. In 1937 he received amnesty and was sent to solitary confinement at Ventotene. After his release in August 1943, he became actively involved in the Resistance. Member of the Consulta in 1945, elected to the Constituent Assembly in 1946, he was president of the latter from February 1947 to May 1948. The same year he was elected senator and was Chairman of the Communist group in the Senate.

TOGLIATTI, PALMIRO (1893-1964). After graduating from law school in Turin, he joined socialism at a very young age. He was among the promoters of *Ordine Nuovo* and the founders of the Italian Communist Party. During the following years, he took part in the internal struggles of the PCI, which—with the Lyon Congress of 1926—ended with the assertion of Gramsci's group. Arrested several times during the fascist regime, he was abroad when the regime promulgated extraordinary laws that led to the arrest and conviction of many Communist leaders. He took over the party leadership and became general secretary. In 1935, during the Seventh Congress of the Communist International, together with G. Dimitrov, he laid down the basis for a unified policy against fascism, which eventually developed into the "popular fronts." He was in Spain during the Civil War, in 1937-1939, as secretary of the Comintern. Later he went to France and then the Soviet Union. He returned to Italy in 1944. He was minister without portfolio in the Badoglio and Bonomi governments; vice-premier in the second Bonomi government; justice minister with Parri; and in the first De Gasperi government. Moving subsequently to the opposition, he was deputy from 1948 and president of the Communist group in parliament.

TROTSKY, LEON [pseudonym of Lev Davidovich Bronstein] (1879–1940). He was among the major exponents of Bolshevism. After the October Revolution, he was People's Commissar for Foreign Affairs and signed the Brest-Litovsk peace treaty. Founder of the Red Army, which he led during the Civil War. Because of his opposition to Stalin, he was expelled from the party in 1927, and went into exile in Turkey, France, Norway, and finally Mexico, where he was murdered by a Soviet agent. Founder of the Fourth International, he continued his tenacious fight against Stalinism. His works include: *My Life* (1930), *Permanent Revolution* (1930), *History of the Russian Revolution* (1932), and *The Revolution Betrayed* (1937).

TURATI, FILIPPO (1857–1932). He was among the founders of the Italian Socialist Party in 1892. He had published the review *Critica sociale* [Social Critique], the theoretical organ of reformed socialism. Deputy since 1896, he was a gradualist, and during Giolitti's decade his politics were largely asserted in the party and trade unions. After World War I, he was the head of the reformist minority of PSI, which gave rise to the United Socialist Party in 1922. An anti-fascist, he emigrated to France in 1926, from where he continued his anti-fascist struggle.

ZINOVIEV [pseudonym of Grigory Yevseevich Radomyslsky] (1883–1936). Russian politician, Lenin's close associate from 1903. Together with Kamenev, he opposed the Bolsheviks' decision to take power. Nevertheless, he continued to be one of the most important leaders of the Communist Party, and in 1919 he was elected president of the Third International. In 1925, he headed the left opposition with Kamenev. In 1932 he was expelled from the party and imprisoned in 1935. He was tried and executed in 1936.

Notes

PREFACE
1.   Antonio A. Santucci, *Senza Comunismo. Labriola, Gramsci, Marx.*
      (Roma: Editori Riuniti 2001).

EDITOR'S NOTE: THE "SPIRIT OF SCISSION"
1.   This is also available online at http://www.internationalgramscisoci-
      ety.org/igsn/pdf/igsn_14.pdf. Retrieved January 19, 2010.
2.   This conference took place in Santiago on May 25–31, 1987, with the
      support of the Gramsci Institute in Rome.
3.   These are akin to the educational equivalent of college, rather than
      high school. [Translator's note.]
4.   *Without Communism* was republished by Editori Riuniti in 2001.
5.   Livio Sichirollo was professor of history of ancient philosophy, most
      recently at the Università di Urbino, before he passed away on April
      4, 2002. His major scholarly contributions centered on the issue of
      dialectics in ancient and modern philosophies. He was also an active
      member of the Communist Party and involved in the local govern-
      ment of Urbino. [Translator's note.]
6.   "Modern Times: Gramsci and the Critique of Americanism," Rome,
      November 20–22, 1987.

INTRODUCTION
1.   Gendered language has been retained to render translation as close to
      the original as possible. The issue of representation, in the linguistic
      sense, has only recently entered academic and activist debates in Italy.
      [Translator's note.]

2. Benedetto Croce (1866–1952) was a major proponent of classical lib-
    eralism as well as a politically active and influential philosopher and
    historian. [Translator's note.]

THE POLITICAL WRITINGS
1. These are Santucci's italics. [Translator's note.]
2. Translation of original text from Karl Marx, *A Contribution to the
    Critique of Political Economy*, Progress Publishers, Moscow,
    1859/1977, http://www.marxists.org/archive/marx/works/1859/cri-
    tique-pol-economy/preface.htm. Retrieved on January 18, 2010.
3. Translation of original text from Karl Marx, Preface to the first
    German edition of *Capital*, Volume 1. Progress Publishers, Moscow,
    1867/1977, http://www.marxists.org/archive/marx/works/1867-
    c1/p1.htm. Retrieved on January 18, 2010.
4. Lenin, V. I., 1920. Speech on the Terms of Admission into the
    Communist International, July 30. In *Collected Works*, 4th English
    Edition, translated by Julius Katzer, Progress Publishers, Moscow,
    1965, Volume 31, pp. 213–263. The text is also available at
    http://marxists.anu.edu.au/archive/lenin/works/1920/jul/x03.htm.
    Retrieved on January 18, 2010.
5. Lenin, V. I., 1920. Speech on Parliamentarism, August 2. In *Collected
    Works*, 4th English Edition, translated by Julius Katzer, Progress
    Publishers, Moscow, 1965, Volume 31, pp. 213–263. The text is also
    available at http://marxists.anu.edu.au/archive/lenin/works/1920/jul/
    x03.htm. Retrieved on January 18, 2010.

THE *PRISON NOTEBOOKS*
1. Sicco Ricci (1375–1447), nicknamed "Polenton" by his father, was a
    jurist and Renaissance humanist punctiliously dedicated to studying
    literature and history in its original Latin. [Translator's note.]

END-OF-CENTURY GRAMSCI
This chapter first appeared in 1996 and the historical and political
events mentioned in the text relate to the years 1989–1996.
1. Translator's note.
2. The Democratic Party of the Left then became the Left Democrats
    [*Democratici di sinistra*] under D'Alema in 1998, fused with some
    center-left parties and currents. In 2007, the Left Democrats, under
    the influence of the centrist currents and allied parties, became part of
    what is now the Democratic Party [*Partito Democratico*].
    [Translator's note.]
3. V. Gerratana, *"Sulla 'classicità' di Gramsci"* [On Gramsci's

"Classicism"] in *Bollettino filosofico*, Department of Philosophy of the University of Calabria, no. 10, 1992, p. 181.

4.   H. Stuart Hughes, *Coscienza e società* [Conscience and Society], Turin, 1979, p. 105.

5.   J. Benda, *Il tradimento dei chierici* [The Clerics' Betrayal], Turin, 1976.

6.   M. Foucault, *Microfisica del potere* [Microphysics of Power], Turin, 1982, pp. 27–28.

7.   E. W. Said, *Dire la verità. Gli intellettuali e il potere* [Telling the Truth: Intellectuals and Power], Milan, 1995, p. 104.

8.   J. P. Sartre, "*In difesa degli intellettuali*" [In Defense of Intellectuals], in *L'universale singolare* [Singular Universal], Milan, 1980, p. 53.

9.   H. Arendt, *Verità e politica* [Truth and Politics], Turin, 1995, pp. 29–30.

10.   H. Arendt, ibid., pp. 34–35.

11.   V. Gerratana, "*Il concetto di egemonia nell'opera di Gramsci*" [The Concept of Hegemony in Gramsci's Work], in *Antonio Gramsci e il "progresso intellettuale di massa"* [Antonio Gramsci and the "Intellectual Progress of the Masses"], Milan, 1995, p. 147.

12.   M. Gorbachev, *Perestrojka. Il nuovo pensiero per il nostro paese e per il mondo* [Perestroika: A New Way of Thinking for Our Country and the World], Milan, 1987, p. 92.

13.   The original text is unclear, but suggests something like "public participation in decision making has become increasingly marginalized." [Translator's note.]

Index